Transg

Christian.

Human.

Transgender.
Christian.
Human.

Alex Clare-Young

wild goose
publications

www.**ionabooks**.com

Wild Goose Publications
21 Carlton Court, Glasgow G5 9JP, UK
www.ionabooks.com
Wild Goose Publications is the publishing division of the Iona Community.
Scottish Charity No. SC003794. Limited Company Reg. No. SC096243.

ISBN 978-1-84952-688-3
Cover photograph and internal photographs © Alex Clare-Young
(except where otherwise indicated)

The publishers gratefully acknowledge the support of the Drummond Trust,
3 Pitt Terrace, Stirling FK8 2EY in producing this book.

Overseas distribution:
Australia: Willow Connection Pty Ltd, Unit 4A, 3-9 Kenneth Road,
Manly Vale, NSW 2093
New Zealand: Pleroma, Higginson Street, Otane 4170, Central Hawkes Bay
Canada: Novalis/Bayard Publishing & Distribution, 10 Lower Spadina Ave.,
Suite 400, Toronto, Ontario M5V 2Z2

Printed by Bell & Bain, Thornliebank, Glasgow

MIX
Paper from
responsible sources
FSC® C007785

Contents

Dedication

This book is dedicated to Jo Clifford with love, gratitude and respect. Your courageous and skilful writing and acting has inspired and continues to inspire and enable our whole global community to speak the truth to power in love and authenticity.

I also wish to express my thanks and love to my biological and chosen family and, in particular, to my mum, Pam Walker-Young, and my wife, Jo Clare-Young, who have always encouraged me to be true to myself, and both of whom have contributed to this book with honesty, humility and bravery.

'For I tell you that what was hid shall come to light.
For inside us we all have a light, and it's maybe the very
thing that we have been taught to be most ashamed of.
And when you have a light, do you hide it in a closet? No!
You bring it out into the open where everyone can see it and
be glad it exists to shine in the world.'

(from *The Gospel according to Jesus, Queen of Heaven,* by Jo Clifford)

Note

The language of gender identity is rapidly changing, allowing trans people to express themselves. I use the singular, gender-neutral pronoun 'they/them' to describe myself.

This can be confusing at first, but we already often use it without noticing, as in 'Someone forgot their umbrella. I hope they're not getting soaked!'

Foreword, by Rachel Mann

The first time I met Alex, over half a decade ago, it was obvious I was in the company of a very smart, creative and talented person. They were someone who had clearly negotiated the profound inner and outer pressures of being transgender in our often uncomprehending church, as well as a hostile wider world. They had faced challenges many could barely comprehend. In the midst of their wounds and exciting personal discoveries, they had begun to live the kind of authentic life which changes other people's lives for the better. I shall never forget the power of their personal testimony both in private conversation and, on one memorable occasion, delivered in front of several hundred youth workers at a Youth Work Conference. The audience gave them a spontaneous standing ovation, and I felt honoured to share a platform with them. When I heard that Alex was exploring ordained ministry in the United Reformed Church, I was both delighted and unsurprised. Their intelligence, sensitivity and character were obvious. Since then Alex has continued to grow into a sophisticated theologian and serious leader.

Transgender. Christian. Human. represents, then, a culmination of lived wisdom and honest wrestling with the joys and traumas of embodying God's call; not just God's call to ordained ministry, but God's invitation to live our bodies, our lives and our very being as fully as we can. For Alex this means celebrating being trans, Christian and human. In a church culture that is still inclined to act as if anyone under forty is little more than a child, some who read Alex's book may be surprised by the depth and honesty of their insights. They should not be. There is a kind of wisdom and knowledge that only becomes available when one goes back, with determination and hope, to the sources of pain and grace. Alex knows what it is to have faced those sources. The details of their experiences are, on occasions, searing, disturbing and shocking, but Alex handles them with skill and intelligence. In doing so, their particular experiences offer space for people with quite different lived experiences to see the world afresh. *Transgender. Christian. Human.* is not always an easy read, but it is a sensitive one, which negotiates the facts of a life without prurience or flinching.

There have been many memoirs by trans people over the decades, including my own *Dazzling Darkness*, also published by Wild Goose back in 2012. In one sense, Alex's book is part of that tradition. However, it represents a fresh departure as well. Many memoirs have been written by those trans people like me who – for whatever reason – have felt very comfortable fitting in to existing gender binaries. Newer, fresher voices like Alex increasingly question the easy distinction between 'male' and 'female' and have brought insight into ideas of gender and identity. They have thereby shaken up the trans community, into the bargain. Alex's voice, formed through rich Christian and theological accents, speaks up for a biblically nuanced and culturally dynamic understanding of gender. I suspect some who read this book will find this very challenging. I hope so. It is usually out of honest wrestling with tough, well-formed ideas and lived experiences that new ways of going on emerge.

There are several outstanding features of this book. Firstly, it exists as a kind of holy workbook centred on gender, faith and compassion. Alex is – as a pastor and teacher – unafraid to encourage their readers to search and go deeper in a quest for understanding. This makes the book so much more than a memoir and brings leaven our anxious society desperately needs. Alex is a helpful guide in a world where trans kids and wider trans identities are mocked by those who wish to use trans people as a whipping post.

Furthermore, this book takes the risk of allowing some of the significant others in Alex's life to speak and share their experiences of walking with Alex. This is terrific and rare stuff, in which Alex's wife Jo and their mum Pam speak with moving honesty and authenticity. Both take us to the joy, delight and real cost of recognising otherness, within and without, as part of God's gracious economy.

Finally, as a minister, Alex is unafraid of prayer. In one sense, this is hardly surprising. If anyone should be comfortable with prayer and its possibilities it should be pastors and ministers (though too often this is not so!). This book is threaded through with it. Prayer, at its best, acknowledges mystery, gift and grace. This is certainly the case in this book. Prayer really matters in Alex's journey (as in so many deeply honest ones) because to live well is to dare to live in mystery and gift. It is a way of going on that entails a work of recognition – that we are not the source, only God. That is the heart of Alex's story and wisdom as I read it: they have discovered that their fundamental identity as transgender, Christian and human flows from the Living God. It is inspiring, hopeful and real.

Canon Rachel Mann
St Augustine's Day, 2019

Introduction

Then YHWH said, 'It is not good for the human to be alone, I will create a helper to mirror the human.' – Genesis 2.18

Who looks like you do? Who mirrors you? Who do you look up to? Important questions for any person, I guess, but more so for those of us who struggle to find an answer. How would you answer this question? Perhaps you look a little bit like an actor you admire. Maybe you are mirrored by a sibling, or look a bit like a parent, or have found a partner who mirrors your soul. It's possible that you look up to a singer, writer, activist or politician. Many of us find ourselves in the characters of books, or in the protagonist of our favourite series or film. Many of us don't.

As a child, I didn't think that anyone was quite like me. As a young person, I didn't want to be like anyone else. As an adult, the search for a mirroring partner led me to dark, dangerous and, eventually, beautiful places. But the point is that it is not uncomplicated for people like me, trans people, to find someone who looks like we do, to cease to be alone, to locate a helper or a role-model who mirrors us.

I am, as you probably knew when you picked up this book, a trans* person. Trans is an imperfect label that will never quite describe anyone exactly, and it means different things to different people. Labels are, to some extent, necessary though. Especially when we choose them for ourselves. For me, being trans means moving towards a gender that varies from my sex assigned at birth – but more about that later. It also means moving between genders and critiquing the rigidity of gendered systems. But that, too, will have to be unpicked as we continue to travel together.

---

* See the 'Defining terms' section on p114 for explanations of words with an asterisk.

So why am I writing this book? Precisely because I think that the question 'Who looks like you do?' is at the heart of being human. As a Christian, I believe that we are called to live in relationship and continual, open conversation with both those who mirror us, and those who are *other* to us. As a trans person, I have experienced that call to live in relationship and dialogue as both blessing and curse; both injury and cure. I have lived through the pain of feeling that there is no one quite like me and I have lived in the joy of sharing differences and similarities with those who are open to talk about their amazingly diverse life stories.

This book is for both the mirror and the stranger. You are welcome, whoever you are, whatever your story. If you are a trans person, I hope you will find bits and pieces of mirrors in this book. I hope that the fragments of my story that mirror yours will bring you comfort, hope and confidence, and spark your imagination and desire to share something of who you are with others. If you are a cis* person, I hope you will find both mirrors and challenges here. I hope that the fragments of my story that mirror yours help you to understand some of what it means to be trans and that the fragments that needle or challenge you inspire you to be in conversation with the *other*, with people whose voices you might not yet have heard.

Written autobiographically, my story is pretty chronological, but you will notice that distinct themes pop out of each chapter. Let's explore some of those themes, so that you can decide whether you would like to walk alongside me from cover to cover or nip in and out of our journey at the points that spark your imagination or answer (I hope!) some of your burning questions.

Beginnings
Childlike faith. Learning to walk. Growing pains.

These chapters explore my childhood and young adult years. I am a 'child of the manse', so reflections on what it is like to grow up in a ministry family inevitably arise. We will also encounter some of the tricky gendered expectations that children are subject to, which will be questioned and challenged.

The focus then shifts to my teenage years, navigating the rocky paths of high school and the rollercoaster ride of adolescence whilst carrying an increasingly heavy load of difference. Painful relationships, sex, mental health and self-harm are key themes. Please look after yourself and read these chapters when you are ready and safe.

Transforming
Transforming discipleship. Learning to run. Transforming call.

For me, transition and developing discipleship are inextricably intertwined. This section describes the journey into faith and towards transition that was central to my life as a young adult. You will encounter tales of prayer, reading and conversation; of discernment, identity and friendship. Authenticity is at the heart of this journey. Here I start to work out what it really means to be me: transgender, Christian, human.

As I move on to discuss transition in more depth, you will find out more about what it is like to be trans, to come out, and to access medical care. You will also come across stories of friendships broken, rebuilt and sustained; families learning how to live with, and love, each other; and trans people navigating the bureaucratic webs of higher education.

I then shift focus to look at my calling to ministry and the ways in which it is related to my trans identity.

Transformative
Learning to fly. Travelling together. Transforming community.

As I transitioned, God's call grew ever louder. I was growing into myself: I knew who I was called to be, but what was I called to do? This section explores calling and ministry, community and listening. What does it mean to be a trans person called to ministry and is it possible to block out God's insistent call?

Of course, it is impossible to block out the call, and so I began to train for ministry. I am the first openly trans person to train for ministry in the URC, so it is an uncomfortable journey at times, but one through which you will see God's creativity, grace and love shining. You will also meet my wife, whose voice will be heard in the next chapter.

So far you have heard a lot of my voice and, as we draw closer to the end of this story (for now!) I thought I'd give you a break. I share the stories of my mum, Pam, and my wife, Jo, so that they can impart something, in their own words, of what it is like to be the loved one of a trans person. We touch on relationships, change, identity and sexuality as well as Christianity, ministry, expectations and respectability.

Finally, I step away from my story, into their stories and, perhaps, yours as well. I tell the story of some of the communities I have been a part of, and the communities I hope to shape. I wonder if I can be part of your community, and how you might walk with me and other trans people.

Each chapter will end with some questions for further reflection, some group work for you to try out in your family, church or community group, and an opportunity to pray. At the end of this book, you will find some resources to help you on your journey, including a list of definitions. Each word that has an asterisk after it can be found there. So, now you have a bit of a roadmap, it is time to start walking. I am Alex – trans, Christian, human. Will you travel part of the way with me?

Beginnings

*Me as a baby.
I see this photo as
completely genderless.*

*I enjoyed playing on the
beach on Iona; even when
the weather was not ideal!
I just loved the freedom.*

Childlike faith

You create me, inside out. (Inspired by Psalm 139)

My happiest memories of childhood are scenes from Iona, where I stayed annually with my family and a group from our church. Four moments stand out: running from the MacLeod Centre to the Abbey, joyfully free and safe; crawling under fences with three, usually very 'proper', ladies from church, when we got lost on the way to the beach; being given camera-film maracas by John Bell, so that I could join in as the only child at music week; and reading my first-ever prayer to a full abbey, in which I thanked God for fish and peas. Life was simple, childlike and fun on Iona. Not so at school.

'Here comes the minister's daughter' to the tune of *Here comes the bride* greeted me every morning for years as I tentatively entered my primary school classroom, dreading the day ahead. Just one of many incidents, thoughts and feelings that convinced me I was an alien in my childhood years. My difference was marked out by belittling songs and chants, social exclusion, the signed list of things that the 'other girls' hated about me and the constant attempts to get me into trouble. It wasn't just the little things, you see. Every isolating incident escalated exponentially, adding to my overwhelming loneliness.

The songs and chants weren't random; they were a mirror held up to show me that I, the shy, stuttering, geeky child of a Church of Scotland minister, was just plain weird. The exclusion didn't just hurt, it led to detentions because I read my book in the corridors or practised the recorder on a bench instead of joining the others in playground games. The list that they made me sign wasn't just childhood teasing; as I signed it, I accepted that my apparently masculine traits, social skills and interests were not acceptable – I was not acceptable. The attempts to get me into trouble worked.

I didn't in fact punch Sofia in the stomach, as my teachers and peers claimed. Rather, I accidentally knocked her as I struggled out of the grip she held on my wrists to keep me from running away whilst the others stood in a suffocating circle and taunted me, occasionally darting into the centre to pull up my skirt. When I told my mum about this incident, aged 25, she was shocked to realise that her understanding of her 'daughter' had been wrong. I wasn't a bad child; they had just made me look like one.

Many children are bullied, and all bullying is bad. It hurts because it is specific. As much as some might say that 'children are just cruel' or 'sticks and stones may break my bones, but words will never hurt me', words do hurt, because they target the core of who we are. I wasn't bullied because children are cruel; I was bullied because I did not conform to the expectations and stereotypes enforced on girls.

At home, the gender dysphoria* was obvious, though neither I nor my parents recognised it as what it was until some years later. The most obvious difficulties were with clothing. I hated my school dress and my Sunday best. I always felt naked somehow. Too visible. I didn't know that it was gender that was the issue; I just felt squirmy inside, not quite right. As soon as I got home I would fling off my dress, pull on a tracksuit and often hide either under my desk or in bed. It always took time to feel safe and comfortable again after wearing a dress.

Clothes shopping was a nightmare too. I remember one trip to Gap in particular. There were two round tables in the middle of the store, both piled up high with hoodies. One table was glaringly pastel: hoodies in pink, purple, pale blue, even yellow. The words were in white and had pretty glittery threads marking out the borders. The other table was bold: hoodies in red, navy, grey and black with black, navy and cream words. I gravitated naturally towards the bold colours until I felt my younger sister tugging on my sleeve. 'Stop being so embarrassing,' she whispered. 'Those are the boys' ones.' My cheeks flushed with shame and rage and I struggled to breathe, descending into a screaming, crying melt-down, a space in which I spent much of my childhood.

She hadn't meant to hurt me. In a way *she* hadn't caused the pain. The norms had. The same norms that made my dresses feel too light, my hair itchingly, achingly long and my feelings incompre-hensible. In my childish mind, she was normal. It was me that was the alien.

I really did feel like I was an alien as a child. When I talk in schools and youth groups I start with the words, 'I wasn't a girl, I was an alien.' It sounds funny, but it's not. Imagine constantly feel-ing as if your clothes are invisible, making you feel more naked than clothed. Imagine listening to everyone around you talking about makeup and boys and shopping and feeling as if every single word is in another language. Imagine being terrified of sleepovers, bathrooms and changing rooms because your body feels like an enemy. Imagine wondering when you are going to disappear, so that you can be replaced by a 'normal' person.

My body became stranger and stranger to me as I grew up. As much as we might prefer otherwise, being trans is about bodies, even when one is a child. Three incidents are burned into my memory. They might be tricky to read about.

The first time my body really betrayed me, I was nine. We had just had swimming class, always an ordeal, and I was in the changing rooms. As usual, I huddled by myself in a corner, towel wrapped tight around my skinny body, trying to make myself as small as possible. My discomfort rapidly turned to panic when I couldn't find my underwear. Struggling to breathe, I pulled my flimsy dress over my head, extricating my towel from under it. The short walk back to school felt like miles as the wind repeatedly whipped up the front of my dress when I held the back and the back when I held the front. From the cool breeze to the giggles around me, I felt completely exposed and humiliated. This experience would be uncomfortable for anyone. To me it was devastating.

The giggles continued throughout the next class, as I sat on the cold, hard chair, distinctly aware of my nudity. At lunch, I rushed to the toilet in tears, to find my pants taped to the window with two sanitary towels, the word 'freak' written on them in thick black marker. I walked home that day acutely aware of the ink bleeding through my pants against my skin. When I got home, I hid the pants in my bag so that I could throw them out the next day. I pulled on three pairs of knickers, a pair of shorts, and my joggers, and hid under my desk until it was dinner time, chanting under my breath, 'This isn't my body, this isn't my body, this isn't my body ...'

The next body incident that I remember is when I was eleven and my period started. I knew that it was going to happen, but I still wasn't prepared. Even now I recall the heat between my legs, the mess and the shame. But, more achingly, I remember the pain in my womb. It was the first time that I became aware of what felt like a hole inside of me. A black, empty fullness that was not part of me, that wasn't supposed to be there. I tried to argue to go home; that I was ill, I was bleeding, I couldn't do this. I lost the argument and sat on the benches in my short sports skirt as the girls played hockey, feeling as if my very centre was being split in two. I was broken.

That brokenness came to the surface that very night, in a third moment that will never leave me; the moment that foreshadowed the self-harming* habit I would later develop. I lay in bed repeatedly stabbing my abdomen and thighs with a drawing pin, and eventually carving the words 'mum' and 'help' into my skin; words which are still faintly visible today; spindly white lines that mark out my brokenness, my humanness, my loss of dignity, of innocence, of childhood.

For much of my childhood years I hid in obsessions: music, collecting, reading. Each of these activities was incredibly good for me. I loved playing my clarsach (folk harp), practising, composing and improvising, and was fortunate to have many exciting experiences including winning prizes at local and national competitions and performing in special places such as the Scottish Parliament and Roslin Chapel. My collections, including Beanie Babies, stamps and coins, taught me diligence and also gained me a prized Brownies' badge. My reading advanced at a rapid pace, allowing me to inhabit marvellous, weird and wonderful worlds and improve my literacy skills at the same time. They were still obsessions though. Coping mechanisms that distracted me from the 'real world' and that I would crumble without.

I also had faith. Me and God were good, even when me and church weren't. We talked pretty much all of the time. Perhaps even then I somehow knew that, in words inspired by Psalm 139, God created me, inside out. Inside out embodiment* is at the heart of my theology, and shapes my understanding of what it is like to grow up trans. Let's go deeper into the words.

O Lord, you have searched me and known me. (Psalm 139.1)

These words are a retrospective blanket wrapped around my childhood isolation. They are like a tight hug, a warming fire, or a comforting drink of hot cocoa. Trans children are not alone. They are known and loved by God. God searches within each one of us and knows us, even when we do not yet know ourselves. Parents cannot be God, but perhaps they might learn from this all-encompassing example of parenthood. Search within your children and know them. But, like God, *Abba*, search and know the little beings whom you have created warmly, lovingly. Look into their eyes, into minds and souls still being formed, still being created, and seek all that is lovely therein.

Treatment of transgender* children is a controversial topic; one which leads to dramatic newspaper headlines and intense online debates. It doesn't have to be, though. Children are resilient and live in a state of constant transformation. Contrary to what many headlines suggest, children in the UK who show gender nonconformity* will not be medicated or immediately categorised. Rather, parents are supported to help children to explore who they are in nuanced, flexible and helpful ways. If your boyish girl grows up to be a tomboy, that's ok. If your feminine boy grows up to be a feminine man, that's ok. If they grow up to be trans, it will be ok.

Gender-nonconforming children do need support, though. When your child complains that their clothes itch, dig deeper to work out what they would rather wear. When their body hurts, help them to separate out real and phantom pain*, to discern what is real, and to find healing. Your GP might be able to help here with a referral to a gender specialist*, particularly if your child rejects gendered clothes or expresses genital discomfort. If your child doesn't like their name, as much as it might hurt you, try to listen with them for the name that God is calling them to use, and affirm that name if you can. For example, if I was your child, you might affirm me by saying, 'God knows the real you, Alex. You are loved, and I will support you whoever you grow up to be.'

> *Even before a word is on my tongue*
> *O Lord, you know it completely.*
> *Such knowledge is too wonderful for me;*

it is so high that I cannot attain it.
(Psalm 139:4-6)

It can be hard to know how to react, whether you are a parent or a teacher, a youth worker or a minister, when a child comes out as trans or expresses discomfort with their gender or with their body. Remember, though, that you are not alone. You are not the first one to hear their disclosure, God is. Try not to question the truth of a child's statement. If a child says that they are a boy, or 'definitely not' a boy, a girl or not a girl, take their word for it. I am what I am. God knows my words are my truth. We can't possibly know or understand the truths that lie beneath a child's words.

A good first step is to accept their words and move forward, trusting that there are truths too big and complicated for us to understand right now. Try saying something like this: 'OK Alex, I hear you. You are not a girl. That's ok. Why don't you try to explain to me? Tell me how I can help.'

For it was you who formed my inward parts;
   you knit me together in my mother's womb.
I praise you, for I am fearfully and wonderfully made.
   Wonderful are your works;
that I know very well.
  My frame was not hidden from you,
when I was being made in secret,
   intricately woven in the depths of the earth.
Your eyes beheld my unformed substance.
In your book were written
   all the days that were formed for me,
   when none of them as yet existed.
  How weighty to me are your thoughts, O God!
   How vast is the sum of them!

> *I try to count them – they are more than the sand;*
>   *I come to the end – I am still with you.*
> (Psalm 139:13-18)

There is a common assumption that all trans people hate their bodies. This is simply not true. Our relationships with our bodies, particularly as we grow up, are complicated and individual. For a time, parts of my body caused me significant discomfort. But I also loved parts of it. My hands were strong, and I could express everything that I felt and much of what others felt by gently caressing the strings of my clarsach (folk harp). My right eye had (and still has) a little brown stripe in the top which made me feel special. I loved to hug and to sing and to swim. Just because my body hurt, just because I hurt my body, did not mean that I hated it. I love my body, but I also love being who God has called me to be, and that is an inside out being; not defined solely by embodiment.

But when I was a child, I was an alien. Who were you?

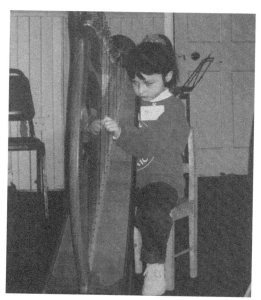

This is the earliest photo I have of myself playing the clarsach (folk harp). I look very focused!

Questions for reflection

- Do you remember how you felt about clothes as a child?
- Can you recall a time in your life when you felt alienated?
- How do you support children in their developing identities?
- What could you consider doing differently?

Activity for groups

- Ask people to write down all of the toys or games that they can think of on post-it notes (one per note).
- Write 'girl' on one large sheet of paper and 'boy' on another.
- Ask people to categorise the toys and games. No matter how difficult it is, they have to go on one sheet or the other.
- Chat about it. Was it easy or difficult? Why did people make the choices that they did?
- Finally, talk about whether any of the toys or games actually need to be categorised?

Prayer

God our parent,
you created and continue to create us, from the inside out.
You knit us together and are still knitting,
stitches that spiral out from the centre, reaching towards the other.
Help us as we share in the crafting of young lives.
Be on our lips as we enter into tricky and precious conversations.
Be in our hands as we attempt to show love and care.
Be with our children as they grow into the people
whom you call them to be.
Creating God, hear our prayer.
Amen.

Playing mini golf in my favourite tracksuit. I enjoyed relaxed days when I felt that I could dress as I wished.

Driving a boat when I was around 10 or 11. This was when I was starting to feel really unhappy.

Learning to walk

You're a young person, full of life; don't let anyone look down on you for that. (Inspired by 1 Tim. 4.12)

If my childhood was characterised by the label 'alien', in my teenage years I was alternately 'freak', 'geek' and 'rebel', depending on whom you asked and how I was feeling. These were the years of escalating bullying, the start of my academic career and the period of rebellion that almost tore me, and my family, apart. This was also when I started to work out who I was. These years were alternately depressing and hilarious, anxiety-riddled and fun-filled, confusing and clarifying.

At twelve years old, the start of secondary school in Scotland, I moved to a mixed-gender comprehensive school, where I spent my days with boys my own age for the first time. There was an immediate sense of recognition. I wanted to look like one of them; I wanted to be one of them; I felt like one of them; I *was* one of them. It became obvious to me that I was supposed to be a boy.

The problem was that this glorious recognition came with an unhealthy side-dose of dysphoria. For the first time ever, my sense of alienation turned into a strong suspicion that I was seriously unwell; that something was badly wrong with me. This idea that I might be a boy was unacceptable and must be hidden, regardless of the cost.

Whilst LGBT+ identities* were starting to be accepted as I was growing up in the '90s and '00s, trans identities were still largely invisible. I saw people in the streets from time to time who my parents told me were 'men dressed as women'. I now realise that they were probably trans people, like me. At the time, though, I didn't know that trans people existed. All I knew (incorrectly) was that some men wore dresses. This didn't connect with my sense of who I was.

The other kids at school thought they knew who I was. 'Weirdo. You shouldn't be in here!' Just one of the many shouted insults that followed me around high school. This particular one was shouted by a group in the girls' toilets, right before they threw raw chicken over the stall door. It landed in my underwear, causing me to throw up and skip class for the rest of the afternoon; just a typical school day for my thirteen-year-old self. In retrospect it is kind of funny. Why did they have raw meat in their school bags, for a start? At the time, though, it was pretty distressing.

Instead of coming out as trans, an option that might have been transformative had it been apparent, I went to lengths to hide my identity. These lengths began with an abusive relationship, took me through a period of severe mental illness, and ultimately led to my coming out as a gay woman just a year or so before leaving school.

Mick (not his real name) was my first big mistake. I was driven to fit in, as I would be again at the start of university – but more on that later. I wanted to seem and act as normal as possible. And, where I was living at the time, the normal for a tweenager was goth. I was twelve years old when I met Mick and his friends, who were all in their early teens. I found that they accepted me, seemingly unconditionally, and felt like I belonged for the first time in my life. The price soon became clear.

I will never forget the first time that I saw self-harm wounds. Mick was rolling down his sleeves as he stalked out of the toilets at the bowling alley, but not quick enough for me to miss the criss-crossed scars which covered his arm. People self-harm for lots of different reasons but for me, at least at first, it came down to bore-dom and admiration. Mick was cool. I was bored. Why not try it?

I swam down into a dark, hazy whirlpool of depression, anxiety, self-harm, drinking and smoking. All secret, of course. The waters were tumultuous, but I fitted in, and that was all I wanted. I knew I wasn't happy, but I didn't think happiness was possible for me, so this would do. The problem is that who I was trying to be wasn't who I really was. It was just another mask. I wasn't Chloé, the depressed and anxious teen girl who cut herself because her friends did; drank and smoked because it was cool. I was Alex, a gloriously geeky teen boy who loved reading, music, public speaking and debate; I just didn't know it yet.

When I wasn't working hard to get top grades at school, or out gigging with my harp, I was with Mick and the gang, hanging out in the woods or in whoever's home happened to be empty, or at youth group. We would drink cheap cider and whisky, smoke rollies, sing along to emo/goth bands and compare scars. I don't mean to trivialise – it all sounds very clichéd, but this was real. This was my life. And it was not good. I hated the taste of cider and rollies, couldn't stand the loud music we listened to and agonised over the permanence of the scars I was creating. I knew that I was self-destructing, but I didn't know how to stop.

Whilst I was able to hide my physical dysphoria in the baggy jeans and hoodies that were a part of our subculture, it was still more than obvious that I was seen as female. One day events tipped just beyond my control, as I lost a game of cards and was dared to take off all my clothes and go up onto the top bunk of my friend's bed with Mick, who touched and kissed me for the first time whilst everyone else giggled below.

Soon Mick and I were entangled in a messy relationship, which felt thrilling with a deep undercurrent of discomfort. Every time he touched me, or kissed me, or even looked at me a certain way, my stomach rolled, and my head ached. This wasn't quite right.

And it wasn't just discomfort. Mick was actively abusive, pushing me to do things I didn't want. But the thing is that the body can be used as a tool; a powerful tool; a tool that assists conformity. I used my female body to fit in, allowing myself to be hurt in order to get through life.

Things spiralled completely out of control one day when, in the middle of a school afternoon, I was interrupted by a text from Mick. He told me that he was in the woods, and that he would kill himself if I didn't come see him immediately. I stammered an excuse to my teacher and ran out of the room, jumped on a bus, and rushed to meet him.

When Mick met me off the bus, he seemed bizarrely OK. Something was wrong though. Despite the fact that it was a dreich, dark, rainy day he insisted that I come with him into the woods and set off at such a pace that I had to follow. What happened after that comes in bits and pieces and is, perhaps, too dark to share in any depth here. When I arrived home that night, I was soaking wet, shivering with cold and fear, and covered up to my knees in mud. I ran upstairs, tore off my clothes, shoved them into a bin bag, pulled on layers and layers of clothes and wrapped myself in a blanket before curling up under my desk where I stayed for hours, sobbing. I was no longer young or innocent. I had been raped. Something had to give.

With the help of my persevering parents, and not much help at all from the local police who didn't believe me, I started again. I got rid of my dark, shapeless clothes and gothic music, my black eyeliner and struggling friends, and was reborn. This time I would be a 'good girl'. Cue phase two of my troubled teens.

Phase two was better on the surface but, perhaps, worse underneath. I spent hours obsessing over clothes and makeup, ensuring

I looked just right. I studied ridiculously hard, being neurotically perfectionist, determined to keep everyone happy with good grades. I gigged almost daily, and practised for hours, keeping myself busy and playing away the bad memories and demons. I started going to a new church, one that was full of teenagers and cool youth workers and awesome music. On the surface it was all good.

That surfacey mask, however, hid an almost unbearable amount of pain. I was still self-harming regularly and was frequently fainting in school, a phenomenon that countless medical professionals labelled as psychosomatic. Whatever the truth, I was not well.

Whilst it had been my abuse at the hands of Mick that had been the final straw, I feel that the majority of my pain was caused by having to actively hide who I was. Every day I put on a mask and a costume and prayed that I would be able to act normal enough, female enough, that no one would find out that I was really just faking it all.

On the return from a disastrous mission trip to Kenya, where I felt completely ostracised by the other young people and leaders, I became physically unwell. I could barely eat or drink without gagging, was plagued by stomach pain, fainted daily, sometimes more than once, and often struggled to breathe. After what seemed like hundreds of blood tests for malaria and other infectious diseases, I was eventually referred to a psychologist.

I was diagnosed with depression and anxiety, and treated with medications, counselling, breathing exercises and even hypnotherapy. I didn't recover fully until much later, but I did get a bit better. I got to a point where I was able to carry on, and so the charade continued into young adulthood – terrible teens phase three.

Having survived really severe mental illness, I realised that I could no longer pretend to be someone that I was not. Hold on, don't rush ahead, I didn't come out as trans quite yet. Don't forget that I didn't even know what trans was. I did know, though, that I would feel a lot better if I could stop pretending to be so girly. And thanks to Ellen DeGeneres I found a way to do just that.

As Ellen rose to popularity, my mum and I started watching her show together. This, along with late night Scrabble games, sleepy-time muffins and peppermint tea to calm my anxiety, was an effort at some serious mother-child bonding. I was going to be OK. We were going to be OK.

I was fascinated by Ellen, and gradually started to drop little hints into our conversations. 'Mum … don't you think I walk a bit like Ellen?' 'Abigail … do you think Ellen's clothes are cool?' 'Dad … what do you think of the Ellen show?' I was gradually realising that the LGBT+ group of identities might be somewhere that I could find myself, somewhere that I could start to understand who I was. More than anything else, though, I realised that, if I came out as gay, it would be seen as 'normal' to dress and act in a more masculine manner. Stereotypical, yes, but the public perception of lesbians was the perfect mask for the last act of my teenage drama.

It was still a mask though. I wasn't really attracted to girls. In fact, I had no idea who I was attracted to, and little interest in dating and sex. Pretending to like girls, though, helped me to fit in; to hide in plain sight; to live a little more like my true self.

This last stage of my teens was perhaps the healthiest. I got my hair cut short, wore 'boyfriend jeans' and slouchy plaid shirts and 'came out'. I was bravely, openly me, or so I thought. The anxiety, the sadness and the pressure were all still there, but I felt respected and loved and that gave me the strength to get through the last few years of school. There was still the need to conform, though, to be someone who I was not.

Cut to my sixth-year prom. I kept the photo but can't bear to include it here. I have short hair and deathly pale skin. I am wearing a 50s-style short dress in teal and black, my grandmother's costume jewellery, and black, arm-length gloves to cover my scars. My wide, lipsticked smile matches that of my pretty girlfriend, who hangs on to my arm. Looking at that photo, I see a lost boy, hiding in drag*. I felt the same that night, most of which I spent hiding in the toilets or outside smoking to counteract the illicit booze. Whilst my lips grinned, and my voice laughed, my mind screamed out, 'This is not who I am!'

How does all of this relate to 1 Timothy 4? The letter-writer addresses a young Christian, perhaps in his teens, saying:

> *These are the things you must insist on and teach. Let no one despise your youth but set the believers an example in speech and conduct, in love, in faith, in purity. Until I arrive, give attention to the public reading of scripture, to exhorting, to teaching. Do not neglect the gift that is in you, which was given to you through prophecy with the laying on of hands by the council of elders. Put these things into practice, devote yourself to them, so that all may see your progress. Pay close attention to yourself and to your teaching; continue in these things, for in doing this you will save both yourself and your hearers.*
> (1 Tim. 4.11-16)

Here I am struck by the attention the writer pays to identity*. He rightly recognises that the ministry of a young person is bound up in who they are. Timothy is not pressured into being 'normal' or 'respectable'. He is not encouraged to wear a mask. Rather, Timothy is encouraged to find out who he is; not to let others despise his – perhaps youthful and idealistic – identity and to speak the truth.

Two verses, 14 and 16, particularly move me. Moving beyond encouragement, the writer urges Timothy to recognise that he contains a gift and that, by paying attention to that gift in the very midst of his person, he can save himself and others. What an empowering message to pass on to an uncertain young person. What an inspiring message this would have been to hear when I was growing up.

I do not blame individuals for my difficult teens. Lots of different things went wrong, and a lot of them started with me. I do wonder, though, what difference a gospel of encouragement, rather than one of conformity, might have made.

You see, I was not encouraged to be myself. I was ordered, by the norms of society, to be someone else. I was discouraged and put down, taught that my identity was non-existent at worst and not good enough at best. I was not able to find out who I really was or told that my identity was a gift. I had gifts, sure, but who I was was not one of them.

So, what might parents and teachers, youth workers and ministers do differently? Just as in the previous chapter, it comes down to good listening. Who is your young person telling you that they are? How can you encourage them? How can you help them to understand themself, and to find the gifts at the very centre of their identity?

The good news is that trans identities* are much more visible today. Young people are unlikely to think that there is no one out there quite like them, because the likelihood is that they will have seen a trans role model on TV, read about trans people, or even met someone who is trans at school. If you are a teacher or youth leader, you might like to consider inviting LGBT+ role models into your school or youth group to speak to young people, to help them to discern and cherish their identities.

Because of the increased visibility, more and more young people are coming out as trans. This raises two questions. Firstly, are you someone that a young person is likely to come out to as trans? Secondly, do you know what to do if they do?

The answer to the first question is very likely to be yes. If you know or work with young people, someone will come out to you at some point. It is also worth thinking, though, about whether you might like to be someone who young people know it is safe to come out to. Many young people struggle in silence for years because they don't know who they could possibly tell about their identity.

If you would like to support trans young people, let everyone know that you are a safe person to talk to. If you work in a public place, display LGBT+ positive posters, quotes or signs. If you parent, teach or lead, tell your young people that it is ok if they are LGBT+, and that you are there for them if they want to talk. Read up on LGBT+ identities and try to avoid words or actions that will, perhaps unintentionally, hurt LGBT+ young people.

The answer to the second question is not as straightforward, but I do have some dos and don'ts to get you started.

1. DO believe them! Make sure that they know you believe them. An easy way to do this is to echo. If someone says, 'I think I might be trans' or 'I think I'm really a boy,' the responses 'OK, thank you for telling me that you are trans' or 'Cool, I am hearing that you identify as male' both buy you time and reassure your conversation partner of your support.

    DON'T tell anyone that their identity might be a phase, confusion or simply wrong. Don't ask them if they are sure.

2. DO keep it confidential. It can be damaging and potentially dangerous to out trans people without their permission. Reassure your conversation partner that you will keep their identity confidential, unless they would like support to tell someone else, and remind them of the boundaries of confidentiality. You might say something like 'I won't tell anyone else, unless you would like me to help you to tell your parents, but not until you are ready. I would only break confidentiality if I thought you were going to hurt yourself or someone else. This sounds like something we can keep between us for now.'

    DON'T gossip. You might feel the urge to share, believing that others will be able to handle this information and keep it private. However, remember that you do not know all of the circumstances and emotions involved. The more people who know that a person is trans without their permission, the more chance there is that that person might come to harm. If you are concerned about a trans young person, it is better to chat to them about who else they might feel able to tell, and encourage and support them in doing so, than to break their confidence. Of course, you can, and should, get support but please try to do so in a way that respects privacy.

3. DO signpost. Gather and keep a handy list of resources and organisations that can help. You will find some in the back of this book. Consider age-appropriate reading and watching and find out about local LGBT+ organisations. Many groups will welcome a visit from or to schools and youth workers.

    DON'T give unwanted advice. Whilst it is helpful and important to show young people where they can find help, advice about who to tell or when and how to (or not to) transition* is not helpful. Most people who come out to you just want someone to tell. Your role is to listen, believe and affirm.

Those are just a few simple tips. If you would like more support, have a look at the resources at the back of this book, or get in touch. For now, here are some questions and an activity and meditation that may help.

In Kenya, aged 15.

Playing clarsach in Glencoe with a new short haircut.

Questions for reflection

- Were you bullied as a teenager?
- How did you feel about your body?
- Do you know any young people who might be feeling isolated?
- Do you know where/how to seek help and support?

Activity for groups

- Buy three current teen magazines: male, female, and ungendered.
- Cut out some of the articles and the front cover. Remove or cover the name or logo of the magazine.
- Ask people to guess which magazine each article is from and which gender they are marketed for.
- Have a conversation about the effects of advertising and journalism on young people, and the stereotypes that they are subjected to.
- Consider chatting about these with young people and asking them what they think. Make sure that this conversation is supportive and non-judgemental.
- How might your church/school/family/youth group challenge stereotypes and open up conversations about identity?

A meditation on questions, written for teens

This meditation is written to help teens to explore their changing bodies and to relax and be affirmed. It can be altered in order to suit the individual and be fully accessible. It can be helpful to encourage a young person to rewrite this meditation for themself, exploring who they are and how they feel. This meditation should be used with care and support, considering the experiences and unique needs of each person who might use it.

These are my feet. How do they feel? How do I treat them? Where do they go grudgingly and what makes them jiggle with joy? Are they comfortable in my shoes? Can I dust the sand off and leave spaces where I feel unwelcome or unsafe?

I love myself. I am becoming myself. I am loved. I am enough.

These are my legs. How do they feel? How do I treat them? What makes them ache and sting? Is it necessary? Am I growing? Do they do what I wish they would? Am I patient enough with them? Do I feel that they are a part of who I am?

I love myself. I am becoming myself. I am loved. I am enough.

This is my centre. How do I feel? How do I treat myself? Do I force my body into situations or clothes that restrain or hurt it? Has someone else hurt me? Does puberty hurt me? How can I make myself feel whole again? Am I ready to learn to love myself?

I love myself. I am becoming myself. I am loved. I am enough.

These are my arms. How do they feel? How do I treat them? Are they strong and aching? Are they long and gangly? Are they full and soft? Where are they scarred? Have they been broken? What loads do I carry, sometimes unseen?

I love myself. I am becoming myself. I am loved. I am enough.

These are my hands. How do they feel? How do I treat them? Are they agile and quick, or slow and tired? Who do I touch? How do I touch? Do my hands belong to me? What can they do for me? What can they do for others?

I love myself. I am becoming myself. I am loved. I am enough.

This is my head. In here is me. All of my hidden thoughts and feelings. All of my identity, learning and becoming. Seeds that will sprout and grow and change. Some corners are dark, I want to keep them locked; others light, full of joy. This is my face. Is it me or a mask? I can choose. I am choosing. One day, I will able to choose.

I love myself. I am becoming myself. I am loved. I am enough.

Learning to cook at home aged 17. By this time I was presenting in as masculine a way as I could get away with.

Moving into halls – terrified!

Growing pains

When their death-oriented journey reached its lowest point, they crucified the innocent one alongside the guilty. But the innocent said, 'Even though you are my parent, you must forgive them, for they know not what they do.' Hearing this, his oppressors humiliated him yet again. (Inspired by Luke 23.33-34)

'Becoming an adult' is overrated and mythical. Now, at age 27, I refer to completing adult tasks like banking, shopping and housework as 'adulting' and try to enjoy much of life in a childlike fashion. I can often be found enjoying 'adult' colouring and arts and crafts or playing board games with Jo, my wife. As a teenager, though, I was desperately excited about 'growing up'. An impending sense of freedom alongside a need to understand who I really was propelled me into the future.

Leaving school and growing into adulthood is, however, difficult for many people and even more tricky for folk who are unsure as to who exactly they are. I was no exception. My first year at music college was one of the hardest of my life, but it was also a time of incredible growth. By the end of the year I had gained a massive amount of strength and a clear sense of identity. But let's go back to the start.

After a rocky final year at school, I was relieved and excited to be taking up a place at one of the UK's top conservatoires, with a teacher whom I admired and abundant opportunities. It finally felt like life was on the up. Of course, I was nervous about this new phase, but I was also looking forward to finally being able to be myself and to make my own decisions. I thought that my life would be perfectly organised and tidy. I was sure that I would make a good group of friends with whom I could be myself. I was adamant that I would work hard and succeed.

In retrospect, I realise that I had completely underestimated the challenges of leaving home, moving into adulthood and learning to fend for oneself. My vision of the future was a dream, or perhaps another act, one that I simply couldn't keep up.

Some of the difficulties were common, typical. I couldn't cook, and often resorted to baked beans, egg on toast or super-noodles. I didn't know the rules of laundry, even though my mum had told me a thousand times, and inevitably all of my whites ended up pink. I hadn't realised until I left home that suddenly I really would have the power to spend all of my money on chocolate and alcohol if I wanted to and so I also often ended up broke.

These problems are common amongst students and, perhaps, deserve a little more attention. Young people should be learning in school how to cook, do laundry and manage essential paperwork. We should be taught how to budget and plan. Instead, many students leave home and feel completely unprepared for the challenges of 'adult' life.

My real problem was bigger than all of those little things, though. I felt like a boy and, as a result, I simply didn't know how to be. The obvious answer, at the time at least, was to try even harder to be a girl. This had failed in the past, but perhaps I just hadn't been trying hard enough. Perhaps I wasn't a boy. Perhaps I was just really rubbish at being a girl. That was my teenage logic anyway! It might sound hilariously paradoxical, but what else was I to do? I had an overwhelming sense that I wasn't a proper girl, combined with a deeply ingrained understanding that society said that I must be one. I thought that I just had to make more effort, and that eventually it would feel right. Once I had perfected girliness!

I chose to move into a halls flat with three 'other girls' and to do my very best to fit in. This was amplified by my department, which consisted of nine girls when I began my degree. Every night I allowed girls to choose my clothes for me, do my hair and makeup, encourage me to pre-drink (even though I actually hated the out-of-control feeling of being drunk) and drag me along to every event and party. Once more, I was pretending to be someone that I wasn't. There was a lot of fun but, beneath the smiley veneer, there was always a sense of hiddenness, of disappointment and of compromise.

The one compromise that I refused to make was with my sexual identity. I had now identified as lesbian for several years and was determined to keep it that way. I dated several girls, and even began to enjoy it. Others, though, weren't so sure. Throughout my first month at college I used the computer lab every evening, as a way to keep in touch with home and to get some alone time for a few hours. Gradually, I became friends with someone who used the lab. We will call him Rick.

As you may guess, Rick was the second man who seriously hurt me when I was living as female. Rick wasn't a Christian but, like many young men, had grown up with the strong belief that all people are heterosexual, and that women who are not attracted to men simply haven't met the right one. I think that Christianity has to own up to some of the blame for that one. We need to rec-ognise that readings of scripture that enforce heterosexuality are at the root of homophobic misunderstandings and actions.

Gradually, as Rick and I got to know each other, he began to ask increasingly intrusive questions about my sex life. Finally, on October 29th, he said, 'I bet I could turn you straight.'

I laughed it off at the time, completely unaware of just how serious Rick was about 'turning me straight'. Now that I know better, it is a phrase that fills me with revulsion. It is disgusting that there are those who believe that they are so attractive that forcing another individual to have sex with them could change said individual's sexual orientation. That is simply not how identity works. So-called 'corrective rape' and 'sexuality conversion therapy' are, however, sadly still commonplace around the world today.

On October 31st, college held a Halloween party. I attended with my friends, dressed as a zombie. Rick was there too, and had decided to dress as a woman, complete with stilettos and heavy makeup. His costume made me feel a mix of amusement and dread. On the one hand, it was laughable that he had clearly dressed as a woman just to try and persuade me to sleep with him, particularly as his choice of outfit couldn't be further from those of women to whom I was attracted. On the other hand, I was starting to realise just how determined he was. I had a feeling that this could end very badly. And it did.

Much later that night, crying in our shared kitchen as I shakily recounted to a flatmate the assault and rape to which he had subjected me, I realised how foolish I had been. I was not safe. Something had to change. I couldn't go on pretending to be someone who I wasn't, especially when it seemed to make others see me as a victim. It was time to start actively looking for answers; time to work out who I was.

What Rick did to me – what Ricks worldwide do to women, to men and to LGBT+ people every day – was and continues to be horrific and undeniably wrong. Rape is never right, never good and never God's plan. For me, though, it was a crossroads moment. I knew that I was living a lie, and Rick was the catalyst of change. Whilst it might seem strange to correlate one of the worst moments of my life with the positivity of a new start, isn't that the story of redemption?

The cross and the resurrection can be seen as paradigmatic of the relationship between oppression and liberation. New life can only come out of death. Transformation can only come out of stasis. And so one of the most horrific and oppressive events of my life took me to a crossroads, which ultimately led to transition. The easy road would have been to stay on the same path, the one that led only to death and decay. Instead, I took the road less travelled: I journeyed towards new life; towards transformation.

Preparing for an orchestral concert at music college. I am smiling because I was told to. I hated the required concert dress. Trousers were not allowed.

Questions for reflection

- Have you ever realised that you were on a destructive path or hiding your true self?
- Do you, or anyone you know, deny the identities of LGBT+ people?
- If so, why?
- What have been some crossroads in your own life?
- Are you at a crossroads now?

Activity at the crossroads

On the Isle of Iona, there is only one crossroads. When the Iona Community, and visitors to the island, spend a day on pilgrimage they use the crossroads as an opportunity for personal reflection. As we stand at the crossroads, we take a moment to consider where we are, where we have been, and where our continued journey might take us.

This activity, inspired by the Iona crossroads, is an opportunity for personal reflection. Use it when you are at a crossroads, a moment of transition, or when you are trying to understand the crossroads that you witness in the lives of trans people. This activity could also be used by churches or groups trying to discern their future.

- Fold a large piece of paper in four, unfold it again and trace the resulting cross with a pen or pencil [+].
- In the top left quadrant, write some notes on where you are now. In the bottom left quadrant, write some notes on what it would mean to continue on the same path. In the top right quadrant, write some notes on what it would mean to change direction. In the bottom right quadrant, write some prompts as you discern a new path.

- You might like to stop and pray in between each quadrant.

Prayer

God of the here and now, being stuck in one place hurts.
As I stand at the crossroads, help me to see a new path ...
God of the past, I was lost.
As I look back, forgive me, help me to let go ...
God of the future, change is frightening.
Help me to look forward to the future with grace and excitement ...
God of the journey, where next?
Amen.

Transforming

Me with my harp from a photo shoot in early transition. The start of the journey was hard, but I was determined to be myself. Photo credit: Graham Martin

Preparing to go cycling for the first time with my local LGBT+ youth group very near the start of my transition.

Transforming discipleship

God created me, formed me, shaped me and calls out to me, 'Do not fear, for I have redeemed you; I have called you by name; you are mine.' (Inspired by Isaiah 43:1)

In the Christian tradition, transformation always necessitates belonging, membership of a new, transformative community. Christian rites such as baptism, confirmation, marriage, funerals and communion all involve community. We are baptised into the community of God. We are confirmed or brought into membership of a denominational or local community. We are married to another, beginning a new family in the pre-existent family that is our church – both familial and chosen community. Our deaths are recognised and our lives celebrated in community. We share meals together, around a table, as communities and are part of a larger community.

My transformation began with the discovery of two communities which would be, for me, the source of new life. One of those communities was a church, the other a youth group. At this point in my journey, church had sort of dropped out of the equation. I was still in conversation with God, still deeply curious about faith, and still committed to a life of love and justice, but I just didn't see church as part of those conversations, my faith, my life. Church was something to rail against. A conservative, patriarchal institution that served only to oppress and control. This attitude to church wasn't random. I had been hurt by a church that wasn't LGBT+ friendly and had projected that hurt onto all churches. The church in question had told me to leave, in the middle of a service, when they had seen me holding hands with another young person of the same gender.

Whilst it was my intention to detach completely from the church, a surprising, spirit-filled combination of my religious upbringing and my recovery from trauma brought me to the steps of another church, one that served the student community in which I lived. This was a church and a chaplaincy that welcomed all people and was characterised by diversity. I didn't know much about it, though, the first time I walked through the door.

I'm still not sure why I gravitated towards the church that Sunday morning, eight years ago. I guess I had an inkling that the loneliness and pain that I was suffering required healing, and I had a tiny speck of hope left in me that the church could, indeed, offer something of an answer. I was frightened, alone and needed somewhere to go. I wasn't coping. I needed help.

I showed up an hour early, jittery and fidgety, anxious and unsure. I almost left, but I was ushered into the building and offered a cup of coffee. I couldn't turn back now. As the stewards set up for worship I paced in the foyer with the warm cup, nervously anticipating the rejection that I expected to come at any moment.

Instead, a cheerful priest, halfway through robing, found me and steered me to where the church members had created a 'welcome wall'. On it, graffiti-style, those gathered had written messages of welcome. Someone had drawn a heart in rainbow colours and written 'LGBTQ. Beloved. Perfect. Called.' I was flabbergasted. I had never seen anything like this before. I started to cry, stunned by the realisation that there just might be a space in this church for me. I stayed, and that staying transformed my life.

Around the same time as I rediscovered the church, I began coming out as a queer* person at the music college at which I was studying. Queer is a complicated word, and one that I don't use lightly, but, as a reclaimed term, it had the capacity to describe an identity that was, for me, impossible to put into words. I didn't identify particularly strongly as lesbian or bisexual*, and I knew that my difference had more to do with gender than sexuality, and so queer was a grasping, questioning, searching word that allowed me to feel my way towards those like me; those mirroring friends that could help me to discern who I was.

I met someone whom we will call Cam. I didn't know this when I first met him, but Cam is a transman*. I still vividly remember the first time I saw Cam by himself, sitting on a wall outside college. Because he looked shy and socially awkward, I gravitated towards him, sensing something that matched the queer(ies) within me. I remember thinking, 'This is someone like me.' We talked, feeling our way around slippery words, trying to get a sense of each other, and eventually Cam asked if I would like to come along to his youth group that evening. Still unsure of the rhymes and reasons, I said yes without hesitation.

My first visit to the local LGBT+ youth group was unforgettable. Cam introduced me to several people, explaining that they were trans, just like him. My head was exploding with questions and confusion but, at the same time, there was a sense of peace, of homecoming. I didn't understand these unfamiliar identities and processes, but I recognised the people who held them as yet more people like me. Suddenly I was neither alien nor alone. The Genesis creation narratives, when read in Hebrew, carry a sense of 'mirroring' – the second human being created to mirror the first. Here, I finally found my mirrors. I finally came into relationship with other humans who reflected my identity back to me.

I gradually learnt more about trans identities, and the process of transition. I spent hours searching the internet, consulting my new friends, and consulting medical experts. There was a clear and loud click, a bright and bold congruence; an inevitable understanding that this was who I was, who I am. 'I am a transman,' I thought, 'and I can be happy.'

I was, however, also grappling with the formation of a newfound discipleship, and I was in no doubt about the fact that, for me, transition had to be preceded by a process of serious discernment. I was trans, but I still needed to work out how to be trans and Christian. My emotions were a whirlpool of excitement and fear, joy and mourning, anticipation and expectation. My thoughts were a muddle of impatient planning and cautious procrastination. Who did God want me to be?

I began to see a spiritual director, who told me to shut my Bible in a drawer; to stop reading and start talking. This 'cold turkey' approach to scripture is not for everyone at every time, nor can it be permanent. For me, though, still reeling from sexual and spiritual abuse, still struggling to move beyond literal readings of scripture, still believing that the Bible said what the conservative youth-pastors of my teen years had told me it said, a break from scripture allowed me to begin to listen to God.

I brought my thoughts and feelings to God honestly in words and in music, in silence and in shouting, in long walks and in times of intense stillness. Art and creativity were the background for this period of spiritual conversation. And I started to hear God whispering a name, the name that would be my name. Alex.

And, after some time, I opened the Bible again. I read passages as if for the first time. *The nations shall see your vindication, and all the kings your glory; and you shall be called by a new name that the mouth of the Lord will give.* (Isaiah 62:2). *Then the man said, 'You shall no longer be called Jacob, but Israel, for you have striven with God and with humans, and have prevailed.'* (Genesis 32:28). *He brought Simon to Jesus, who looked at him and said, 'You are Simon son of John. You are to be called Cephas' (which is translated Peter).* (John 1:42)

These verses, which had barely been touched upon by my previous pastors, took on new meaning for me. I could be called by 'a new name that the mouth of the Lord will give'. Alex. You shall no longer be called your old name. You have wrestled with me and discerned a new name. Alex. I recognise you. And you are to be called Alex.

Hearing a new name was one thing, saying it quite another. I whispered my new name to Cam, who in turn, with my permission, shared it with the leaders of the youth group. From then on, on Tuesday nights and Saturday mornings, I was Alex. It was an experiment, a try-out of my new life, and it felt great. There were hilarious moments at first, when people said 'Alex' and I failed to respond, forgetting my own name. There was the joy and laughter of trying out new signatures, each as silly as the last. But there was also fear. Here, I could be Alex, but what about out in the real world?

Eventually I told my minister, who accepted my truth with a mixture of grace and curiosity. This was not a conversation that he had been expecting, but he listened carefully, and helped me to tease out the next steps. I wrote a letter to members of the congregation and delivered it with much fear and trembling.

And, one at a time, they responded with much acceptance and love. Brian, who was over eighty years old, wrote me a letter in return, in which he praised my courage and honesty, and invited me over for dinner. And God whispered, 'Do not fear, for I have called you by your name, you are mine.' Ellie, who knew that I had a difficult journey ahead, offered her son's old clothes, to help me to start out. And God whispered, 'Do not fear, for I have called you by your name, you are mine.' Sandra, who had never met a trans person before, took me out for lunch and listened and learned. And God whispered, 'Do not fear, for I have called you by your name, you are mine.'

So, with the help of faithful, generous and loving disciples, my own discipleship was transformed. I was Alex. My journey was just beginning. But I knew that I could do it, with God's help.

Years later, I found out that a couple had left the church when I came out. They disagreed with the minister's decision to accept me. And, in a way, that's ok. I heard one call, and they heard another. God's ways are mysterious, and God's truths are multiple. Let's not feel threatened by the differences held within the body of Christ.

Questions for reflection

- Is your church/school/workplace/youth group a place where a trans person could be enabled to explore, discover and express their identity? If not, why not?
- How would you react if someone came out to you as trans?
- Where, and with whom, are you able to be fully you?
- Who is God calling you to be?
- What would you say to someone who disagreed with your own views?

Activity – spectrums

All you need for this activity is an empty room and a group of people. Each end of the room is a binary position, with the spectrum spreading across the room between the two ends. Encourage people to stand in a line according to their opinion. For example, if one end of the room is yes, the other is no. People will spread out across the room depending on whether their answer is 'yes', 'sort of yes', 'maybe', 'sort of no' or 'no'.

Start with simple, silly questions:

- Sweet or savoury? (If you prefer sweet, go to that end of the room, savoury the other, or perhaps you are somewhere in the middle).
- TV or books?
- Fiction or non-fiction?
- Gryffindor or Slytherin?

And then more serious questions:

- Agree or disagree: God created male and female.
- It's ok to be trans.

- Our church is a safe space to come out.
- And so on …

With each question, encourage people to share their views. This enables the group to grow in empathy, and to understand their differences.

Prayer

Loving God, help us to discern the people that you call us to be.
Help us to discern the community that you draw us into.

Who are we to be?

[Period of quiet reflection]

God says: I have called you by your name, you are mine.
Trust that still, small voice. Amen.

Learning to run

'Not just my feet but my whole body, let me dive straight in!' demanded Simon-Peter in his naive enthusiasm. Jesus answered, 'Those who have had a bath need only to wash their feet; their whole body is clean. And you are clean … Mostly.' (Inspired by John 13:9-10)

When a new, exciting thing is happening, it is very easy to get over-enthusiastic. Transition is no exception. I was so thrilled finally to know who I was called to be, as much as any of us ever do, that I was desperate to jump right in, to do everything, immediately. If someone had offered me the chance to grow a three-foot beard the very next day after coming out, I would have leapt at it.

My enthusiasm came with pluses and minuses. On the one hand, I was ready to jump through the hoops, to do whatever I had to do in order to transition. On the other hand, I expected everyone else to be ready too. In retrospect, that expectation was not realistic. If I had the opportunity to go back and do it all over again, I would give my family and friends a little more time to get to know the real me.

Coming out was a mixed bag. You already know about the fantastic reactions from my youth group and church. But there were a lot more people to tell. Think of all of the hundreds (perhaps thousands!) of people you know, and imagine telling them that you are not the gender they thought you were … Not an easy task or a one size fits all.

Coming out to my family was definitely something that I didn't take enough time over. It was the second time I had had to come out. When I had come out as gay, it had been pretty easy. My parents and sister completely accepted it, and that was that. Coming out again was always going to be hard, because I had to directly contradict myself, and explain how I had come to this new conclusion.

I came out to my dad in person but, because of the timings, wrote to my mum and my sister. That was a mistake. I think I made them feel as though I was rushing a decision and that I didn't care enough about them to talk to them face-to-face. It wasn't surprising, then, that it took them a while to understand and come to terms with my transition.

Now, though, my family are my greatest supporters. My dad chats with me about gender all the time, stretching himself as he journeys alongside me. My mum advocates* tirelessly for trans people and is a passionate ally*. My sister is one of my closest friends, though we live so far apart. Whenever I see her, it is like we have never not been a team.

Coming out to close friends was very difficult. It is tricky for people to understand just how hard trans people work, before transition, to keep our identities a secret. We even lie to ourselves. When I came out, transness was still largely underground, unheard of, and so we hid in the shadows. Explaining to my friends that the girl in dresses and makeup whom they had come to know was not really me was tricky to say the least. Being a professional musician did not help. I had to perform in 'evening dress', which meant dresses for girls and tuxes for guys. There was no middle ground. It's not surprising that some people struggled to understand the sudden change of attire!

It is surprising, though, that people can be so willing to abandon those they care about. I will never forget my best friend saying, 'I was ok with the gay thing, but this is just stupid. Why can't you be normal? It's not for me. Good luck, but goodbye.' In the decade since I came out, I have made amazing new friends and have mourned, and let go of, those I lost. It saddens me, though, that so many trans people are abandoned by family and friends, just because they finally feel able to be open and honest about who they are and how they feel.

The university didn't exactly help either. When I came out, I was asked if it was a phase, and if I had considered having counselling before I told anyone. Then, on the first day of term, I arrived to find that the class lists posted on the corridor wall contained both my names. Alex Young, my correct name, was followed by my previous name in brackets. When I confronted an administrator, I was told that this was so that lecturers would know who I was, and that it could not be changed.

The university was just the first of many organisations that I had to come out to. From the government to banks, from memberships to mailing lists, there are lots of people to come out to. Sometimes it was easy. To change my driving licence, I simply had to fill out an online form and send in a copy of my change of name deed poll and a doctor's letter. Other companies, however, seemed determined to make the process as hard as possible. One bank, for example, refused to change my details, because my voice sounded female on the telephone. Eventually, I had to close my account.

Gatekeeping, the process whereby people in positions of power hold control over an individual, is a big part of life for trans people. I was no exception. One of the hardest battles I faced was to get a Gender Recognition Certificate*. The Gender Recognition Act* is the way in which trans people are legally recognised. Whilst some trans people do not choose to seek legal recognition, many of us feel that it is essential in order to live as a full member of society.

A Gender Recognition Certificate allows one to hold a birth certificate in one's true gender, to complete a DBS check without disclosing one's former name to one's employer, to marry* in one's true gender and to be protected from discrimination, outing, doxing* and transphobic abuse. Without a Gender Recognition Certificate, it would have been incredibly difficult, perhaps impossible, for me to work in the church, marry the woman I love, and feel safe and recognised in the world as the person that I am.

Getting one, though, was far from straightforward. To get a Gender Recognition Certificate, you have to jump through all sorts of hoops including paperwork, proof, doctors' letters and statutory declarations, not to mention the payment of a fee. You then wait while a panel decides whether you qualify. I failed twice before my application was finally accepted, six years into transition.

Transition was also full of joy though. The gift of being called Alex and he and sir for the first times. The peace of shopping for the right clothes. The confidence to speak and pray and preach without stuttering. The sense of fulfilment as my body gradually changed.

Which brings us to the question of medical transition. Medical transition is the thing that trans people get asked about the most. The questions are usually well-meaning, but questions like 'Have you had the op yet?', 'When did you complete your transition?' and 'So are you fully male now?' (usually accompanied by a sneaky glance down) can be really offensive.

These questions seem to imply that our bodies, specifically our genitals, are more important than anything else about us and are open to public scrutiny. I will tell you about my medical transition. Not because I feel that I have to, or that trans people should be open to such public scrutiny. Rather, I feel that, as someone who is very comfortable being open, I can bear some of the burden for my trans siblings by sharing some of our truths and possibilities.

What follows will be quite detailed, so if you are squeamish you might prefer to skip to the end of this chapter. If you do read on, please remember that every person, body and transition is different and that all are worthy of respect and dignity.

The NHS waiting list for transition is incredibly long. After waiting up to five years, trans people must then go through between three months and one year living 'in role', followed by two clinical assessments that might be up to a year apart before they even begin to physically transition. This isn't all down to protocol. An overstretched service is struggling to meet the needs of the many people who finally feel that it is possible and safe to transition. It can take, then, up to eight years to begin to take hormones. And that's if everything goes smoothly.

The system works brilliantly for some people, and a slow transition can be healthy. Personally, I couldn't wait that long, and I have met many others who have struggled with the wait. It doesn't take long on Google (other search engines are available!) to find a long list of people who have chosen to take their own lives, unable to wait. I may have ended up on that list were it not for a kindly, leading NHS gender specialist who, frustrated with a struggling system, chose to set up a private clinic in his spare time. I was one of his first patients and will never cease to be thankful for the opportunity he, and a hefty overdraft, gave me.

Don't get me wrong, I didn't skip the important bits. I had been living as male for six months by the time I registered with the clinic and was certain that transition was right for me. On a cold, wintry day I made the journey down to London and sat anxiously in the small waiting room. I felt like I had waited so long for this moment, and I didn't believe that it could possibly go smoothly. It did though.

The psychologist spent almost two hours uncovering my life story and helping me to sift out the pearls, laboriously untangling them from seaweed and gently cleaning them off. By the end of the session I felt exhausted and emotionally spent, but also affirmed and clear-minded. I knew who I was and what I needed and there was a path for me.

I obtained a second opinion from the psychologist's colleague three months later, allowing him to recommend that my GP prescribe me testosterone, and that I join the NHS waiting list for further treatment. And so the journey began. After a series of blood tests that would become a regular feature of my life, I was finally able to begin the testosterone injections that would soon become routine. It is hard to describe the difference that those injections have made for me.

The visible changes are obvious. Facial and body hair, muscular redistribution* and skin changes, to name but a few. The invisible transformations, though, were greater than I had dared to imagine. I felt healthy and well; I had an appetite, allowing me to reach a healthy weight for the first time in years; I had energy; I felt calm; I felt happy. Who knew that testosterone can have such an impact!

Once on testosterone, I knew that I needed chest surgery. Dysphoria manifests in many ways, one of them being physical pain. I had always had an unreasonable amount of physical pain in my chest tissue and was also very sensitive to touch in my chest area. Even a simple hug hurt. When I transitioned, I began to bind* my chest, which soothed much of the discomfort and pain. Unfortunately, though, binding came with the side effect of exacerbating my asthma. Chest surgery, I knew, would relieve all of my symptoms. This was not just about how I looked, it was also about how I felt.

Binding can be really important to trans people and is rarely just related to appearance. It is, however, expensive to access safe binders. I was fortunate to be able to do so but have also had the horrific experience of taking a young person to A&E to have the duct tape that they had felt they needed to use peeled away from their chest. Much of their skin came away with the tape.

Accessing transition-related surgeries on the NHS is not as straightforward as some media outlets would have you believe. A shortage in qualified and willing surgeons means that waiting lists are very long, and that is after you have had the two Gender Identity Clinic appointments necessary to join the list. Eventually, I was referred to a surgeon, and was very excited to meet her. Our consultation went well, and I was put on a waiting list. Two years later I found out that she had ceased NHS practice, and was only taking on private patients. And so the process began again.

Finally, I was able to have my chest surgery in London and it was a fantastic, if tricky at times, experience. I had peri-areolar surgery*, which is a keyhole technique that allows for minimal scarring. The biggest difficulty was changing bandages and coping with travel immediately after surgery. Once healed, though, the results were better than I ever expected. My chest is now pain and discomfort free. A bonus is that I do not feel afraid to get changed in front of people.

My last gender-related surgery was also medically necessary. The Gender Identity Clinic asked that I be referred for a hysterectomy, because I experienced severe cramping and was at a heightened risk of endometrial thickening and atrophy.

We were all good to go, and I attended a consultation at my local hospital. It was a little awkward to be seen in the women's clinic and to answer personal questions but as far as I was aware, all was well. Later that evening I received a frustrating phone call from the surgeon, stating that my funding had been denied. I wrote a polite but firm complaint letter the next day, outlining the medical reasons for my surgery and asking whether it was perhaps discriminatory to disallow treatment, when it would be offered to any cis person in my situation.

Less than 24 hours later I received a phone call from the manager to apologise and confirm that funding had now been obtained, and to let me know that I was on the waiting list. She explained that the hospital had assumed my surgery was due to 'mental health' and that as soon as physical symptoms were mentioned the funding decision was reversed.

This wasn't the first time I had had difficulties accessing medical treatment. I have had doctors refusing to prescribe my hormones, nurses grumbling about having to administer my injections, paramedics asking me intrusive and irrelevant questions, and physical health problems repeatedly attributed to either my transition or my mental health. I know that my trans friends and colleagues can tell similar stories.

I eventually had my hysterectomy just a few months ago and, having recovered well, see my physical transition as being complete. I am unlikely to have any further surgeries, as they are not something that I want or need. There is no such thing as an endpoint in transition. Rather, each trans person makes the medical decisions that suit them. Some trans people will have no medical treatments, others will have numerous; it is up to the individual.

Medical transition is one of the aspects of trans identity that upsets some Christians, so I would like to write a little about the theology behind this. Much of the discomfort is due to the theological understanding that God is inerrant – God does not make mistakes – and that trans people are claiming that our bodies are a mistake.

But that isn't how many trans people see themselves, myself included. No part of me, neither my identity nor my body, is a mistake. I am a human being, created in God's image, and human bodies change, both naturally and artificially. People grow older, bodies atrophy; this process does not imply error on God's part. People have medical and cosmetic surgeries, which do not imply error on God's part. We have haircuts, wear makeup, and indulge in spa treatments, none of which imply error on God's part. Being human is messy, complex and transformational. I believe that God is a part of all of that.

I have never understood puritanical interpretations of Paul's assertions, in 1 Corinthians, that the body is a temple. The first mention of this phrase is plural, applying to the believers as the body of Christ. The second is individual. If the body is a temple, though, it ought to be adorned and enjoyed. Just remember how ornate God told the Israelites to make the tabernacle during the exodus. Our bodies are miracles, works of art, astounding creations, and should be treated as such. For me, part of respecting and enjoying the body I have been given has been to transition, not to mention the tattoos and piercings with which I have decorated it!

Questions for reflection

- Have you ever had to tell someone something difficult? How did you do it? How might you do it differently next time?
- Has anyone ever come out to you? How did you react? How might you react in future?
- What changes have you made to/experienced in your body? How do you feel about them?
- What are you thankful for in the way that you have been created? How might you celebrate your identity?

Individual activity

- Ask someone to draw around your body.
- Spend some time considering the outline, considering yourself.
- Then adorn your body drawing. Colour, collage, write, draw. This is you. Who are you? Who do you wish to be? Who are you created and recreated as?

Group activity

- Draw a body on a large piece of flipchart paper.
- Adorn it together, considering what each of you lends to the church/community/group and how you wish to continue to shape it.

Prayer

Creating, loving, nurturing and transforming God,
you created and continue to recreate our bodies.

Help us to treat our bodies as a temple,
respecting, adorning and enjoying them,
participating in the work and play of creation.

Help us to treat the bodies of others as temples,
allowing them respect, privacy and autonomy,
participating in the work and play of love.

Help us to treat the body of the church as a temple,
growing our community in respect, nurture and transformation,
participating in the work and play of ecclesia.

Creating, loving, nurturing and transforming God,
be with us in all our daily transitions. Amen.

Transforming call

He told them: 'You can't take anything on the journey – no tools, no bag, no food, no cash, no extra clothes.' (Inspired by Luke 9.3)

At the same time as going through transition, I was also journeying towards calling to ordained ministry. The calling journey, like transition, is long, complex, transformative, a privilege and a struggle. You are asked to leave behind everything you know and step out in faith, not knowing what the future holds. In this chapter I will share a bit about what the calling journey was like for me, particularly as a trans person.

My calling journey started with attending the church referenced in Chapter Four. I went to church twice weekly and was at church events almost every day. Pretty soon, I was being asked to help out, invited to get involved. From filling the chalice, to sharing it, from reading the word, to praying it, I was becoming part of the church, not just attending a church.

About a year in, early in my transition, I was asked to lead a service on/for people with LGBT+ identities. I was stunned, and pretty much laughed out loud. I had never led a service before and didn't really know how to. I was pretty sure that I wasn't capable. I had no self-confidence whatsoever at this point. I knew, though, that it was a privilege to be asked, and I was determined to lead the service, and to lead it well.

I thought carefully about services I had attended, concerts I had curated, and prayers I had appreciated. And then I thought about myself and my LGBT+ friends. 'Who am I? Who are we?' I asked myself. Gaining confidence, I wrote a list of attributes important to the LGBT+ community, and a list of essential elements of worship. Then I got creative, shaping a service that I hoped would help my community to share our joys and our sorrows and would help the church to understand and to commit to welcoming and loving LGBT+ people as part of our fellowship.

Having written the service, and checked through it with my chaplain, it was time to go for it! We set up and waited, and I was shocked when, just before the service was due to begin, I had to put out more chairs. The room was full to bursting and they were waiting for me to get up to the front and take them through the service!

Despite my years of performance experience in the music industry, I was terrified. I was very nervous about talking in front of people, unsure about sharing my own testimony, and aware that the participants had all come for different reasons, with different expectations and needs. I didn't know if I could give them what they wanted.

My chaplain said it was time to begin and we walked to the front of the room, where he introduced me and sat down. Shaking, and feeling rather sick, I took a deep breath and began my opening prayer. Immediately, a sense of calm, peace and fulfilment began to spread throughout my body and mind. This was a feeling that I had never before experienced in all my years of performance.

It wasn't until the service was over, the congregation gone, that I stopped to analyse how I was feeling. I approached the chaplain and said tentatively, 'I think I might be called to ministry.' A grin spread over his face as he nodded slowly and said simply, 'Indeed.'

Later that year, having graduated from music college with a 2:1, it was time to start to think seriously about what to do next. I applied for, and was granted, a job as student worker at the chaplaincy, which gave me time to explore my calling. I knew that I was called to a form of ministry but what, or where, was still a mystery to me.

Increasingly, young people are not members of a single church or denomination. In my case, I had been confirmed and brought into membership at a four-way local ecumenical partnership, meaning that I was a member of the United Reformed Church (URC), the Church of England, the Baptist Union and the Methodist Church. The first big decision, then, was denominational.

I read documents and doctrine and spoke with friends who were in ministry. It soon became clear that there was only one denomination that I could feel called to ministry in, the United Reformed Church. The URC's Statement of Faith and Basis of Union were documents that I could agree with wholeheartedly, without having to cross my fingers. I also knew that it was a denomination where I would be relatively safe as a trans person, though my journey would not be straightforward.

I went to visit my moderator, the person who has oversight of an area of the URC, who was very enthusiastic about my sense of call, and who encouraged me to learn more about the URC. I did this in two ways. Firstly, by attending, and occasionally leading worship at, various URC churches and also by completing Training for Learning and Serving (TLS).

Eventually, after an assessed service, church interview, local interview, synod interview and lengthy form-filling, it was time to go to an assessment conference, which would make the decision as to whether I was called to train for ministry. When filling out the forms, I had had to make decisions about how open and honest to be about my identity. I had actually paused the process for a while, when a minister to whom I showed my draft answers had encouraged me to be more conservative. Unsure what to do, I felt that my whole calling had been brought into question. For me, authenticity and integrity are important foundations for ministry. Could I be a minister if my whole self was not welcomed by the church; if I had to lie and hide to do it?

When I returned to the form, I decided to write my truth, even if it might cost me my calling. I wrote about being trans, and about how, for me, my gender identity is woven through my sense of calling. Transformation, change and new life are at the heart of the Gospel and are all facts of life for trans people. I feel that I am called because of, not despite, my transness.

Writing my truth, of course, made the assessment conference a little harder. To be fair, my transness in and of itself was not treated as an issue. Rather, several of the assessors made it clear that they felt that my transness was an important part of my journey, asking me questions about what I had learned about myself and others through my transition. More sceptical assessors, however, used my stage of transition and my age against me. One individual in particular asked very telling questions, starting with, 'But surely you need to be more settled in who you are first?' and concluding with, 'But how can you possibly empathise with, for example, a middle-aged businessman at your age and stage of life?' I answered with dignity, respect and care but did feel that these questions unfairly brought my integrity and life-experiences into question.

Thomas Merton famously said, 'Our job is to love others without stopping to inquire whether or not they are worthy.' By refusing to ever 'settle' in a concrete form of identity, I am able to love anyone, regardless of where they are in life or what their beliefs are. I can empathise with pretty much anyone because of, not despite, my trans journey, which has taught me that everyone is worthy of love. I have lived a lot in my 27 years and have come to understand that people are just people, whatever their identities and beliefs, and that I love people. Unconditionally.

What I had yet to learn, at the start of my calling journey, was how to love myself unconditionally. That one assessor's concerns weighed on me to such an extent that I did not believe I would be accepted to train for ministry. I didn't think I would be seen as good enough. I guess, in reality, I doubted whether I really was good enough. But I was wrong. I was accepted to train. I was at another crossroads, ready to begin a new adventure.

My gender identity was a feature throughout my training, in both troubling and exciting ways. When I went to visit the colleges, to help me consider where to train, I asked the principals how my gender identity would be received. The principal of the college I chose to train at was clear that my identity was not an issue but, rather, a gift; that it was my choice when and if I talked about it and that, if I did, it would be received as a blessing. This allayed some, if not all, of my fears about being the first openly transgender ordinand in the URC.

Fast forward six months and I was starting at college, completely unsure of how I would be received but also pretty certain that I wouldn't find anyone like me there. How very wrong I was. Theological college was, and continues to be, a place where diverse, interesting, often wounded and always courageous people come together to talk about God and to prepare to walk God's way in the world. Little did I know that I would also meet my wife, Jo, at college.

Jo and I became friends very quickly and often sat up into the early hours drinking whisky and playing board games in the common room or having in-depth theological debates in one or other of our rooms. Unfortunately, this caused quite a lot of consternation. All sorts of reasons were given for people's concerns but, at the heart of it, was the assumption that we were sleeping together. I don't think that any overt transphobia was at play, but I do think that it is interesting that promiscuity is assumed of

LGBT+ people more readily than of others. Many others spent similar amounts of time together in their rooms, but they were heterosexual, and therefore not under suspicion.

Nevertheless, our friendship blossomed and after only a few months, with the full support of college, we discerned a call to marriage. Our wedding, like our identities, was not conventional. Neither of us was entirely sure what we felt about church marriage, given that marriage is increasingly a function of the state. Further, we were keenly aware of the challenges for LGBT+ people of getting married in church, despite our denomination's conditional acceptance. In the end, we opted for a registry office marriage, followed by a religious blessing at an old chapel which is being converted into a retreat centre for LGBT+ people by a good friend of ours.

Our blessing was a casual one, with a small number of close friends and family gathered together around words, prayers, music and hospitality. We wrote much of the liturgy ourselves as we were keen to ensure that what we said in front of God and our loved ones truly reflected what we believed and felt. We re-read those words together each year on our anniversary, and they still ring true.

It just so happens that, on the bookshelf at that very retreat centre, I came across *The Gospel According to Jesus, Queen of Heaven*. The powerful words of Jo Clifford spoke to me and I began to wonder about my calling. Was I called to ministry in and of itself, or was I specifically called to ministry as a trans person? As someone who could share the love of God with people from my understanding of what it meant to be transgender, Christian, human?

Looking back, it is clear that this was a turning point in my calling journey, and my life. I went back to college determined to be more open about my transness, and to consider what impact my identity might have theologically. I wrote a dissertation that year on translations of gender in the Genesis creation narratives, having learned rudimentary Hebrew the previous year. I was determined to understand why people thought that the biblical text mandated binary gender, when I was so sure it didn't.

That essay received one of my highest marks, and I began to be invited to speak about gender identity at conferences. I led training and blogged, and met with trans people and sceptics, feeling increasingly called to share the good news of transformation that I had experienced in my life, and seen in the lives of so many others.

Whilst I had been unsure of my academic ability in the first year of my undergraduate degree, by the second year my passion for trans theology* led me to apply for a masters. I was accepted and absolutely loved the experience, thriving on academic and pastoral debate and conversations about the nature of God and of humanity. I finished my MPhil with a thesis entitled 'Towards a Transgender Theology of Personhood' and conference experience as far afield as Mexico City!

I am now in my final year of training for ministry, and my calling journey continues to loop back to gender identity. I spend hours every day blogging and writing about trans theology and responding to questions from students, ministers and trans people who need support and community. Trans people have been writing trans theology for decades, but it is only just starting to be read. Trans people have been in church for millennia, but ministers are only just starting to wonder how best to serve us. Trans people have hidden in closets for years, but we are coming out, and seeking community and fellowship.

Where will this journey towards ministry lead? Who knows. One thing I have learned over the years is that trying to guess God's plan is foolish. What I do know is that my gender identity is a gift and is part of my calling.

Wearing a t-shirt with a trans-visibility statement. I love wearing this kind of thing now, but wouldn't have dared in my early transition.

On Iona in 2015 as I prepared to begin my training for ministry.

Questions

- What is your vocation?
- Do you/how do you experience a sense of God's call in your life?
- What questions would you like to ask those who minister to you?
- What questions would you like to ask trans people?

Activity – meeting around the tables

It is often difficult to have open and honest conversations about trans identities, for fear of offending people, because of concern about political correctness, or simply not knowing where to start. For this activity, it is best if trans people aren't present. That makes is a safe place for cis people to raise questions and express opinions.

- Ask members of your group or fellowship to write down all of their questions and/or opinions about trans people, each on a single post-it note. Spread the post-it notes out on a table. Meet together around the table for refreshments or a meal, and use the post-it notes as prompts for conversation.
- Make sure that you set some ground rules together, to ensure that everyone feels safe and able to talk openly, and, if appropriate, you might like to consider praying as you start and finish.
- It might be helpful to ask group members to read this book first, and to write down their questions or comments as they go through. Once you have met and talked, I would be more than happy to answer any questions that you might have.

Prayer based on Psalm 138

I will praise you, God, with all of my being;
    before all else I will sing your praise.
I will come authentically, just as I am, to your holy temple
    and will praise your unfathomable name
    for your unfailing love and your faithfulness,
because you keep your promises.

When I called, you called back;
    you gave me courage.
May all people praise you, God,
    when they hear what you have decreed.
May they sing of the ways of transformation
    for the glory of love is great.

Though you are lifted up, you prioritise those trampled down;
    you see each person's truths.
Though I walk in ways that risk persecution,
    you look after me.
You stretch out your hand against privilege, power and hatred;
    with your right hand you save the oppressed and the persecuted.
The Lord will vindicate those who live their truths;
    your love, God, endures for ever. Amen.

Transformative

Celebrating my 21st birthday in ministerial training college.

Enjoying the days after ordination. It felt like a coming together; an emerging; a new opportunity to be the person whom God has called me to be.

Learning to fly

If people do not welcome me, I will leave their town and shake myself off. I won't overreact or worry about it. I am enough. (Inspired by Luke 9.5)

When I wrote about the start of my calling journey, I mentioned not feeling good enough. I think it had a lot to do with authenticity, or the lack thereof. I felt unable to be completely myself, because I was hiding or downplaying the parts of me that might be inconvenient. Learning to run was about transitioning, about being myself, about allowing myself to be transformed into, well, me! Learning to fly, though, is about living in constant transition, being authentic about myself, and allowing myself to be continually transformed by God without any set end point or goal. I am enough. It's as simple as that.

The journey of training for ministry, and the concurrent adventure of marriage, stripped away my self-doubt and allowed me to start to consider who I *really* was, and how I should not only speak my truth but also love my truth. Having amazing people around me, such as my wife, Jo, who encouraged and emboldened me, allowed me to play with identity and to simply *be*.

My MPhil thesis led me to the conclude that:

The image of God in humanity is, in part, found in our flexibility; our ability to transform and to be transformed in communication with God and with other people.

Reducing people to their bodies is a distortion of that image of God.

Jesus redeems us precisely by bringing us back into communication, by allowing, enabling and encouraging us to listen to, and share our truths with, God and each other.

Identity must, as such, be flexible, not static.

These conclusions mean that trans people can have a missiological role – we can help other people, cis or trans, to understand what it means to be transformed and transformative.

But only if we are open to being transformed and transformative, and to sharing those truths with others. What that meant for me was that pretending a binary identity was limiting the ways in which I lived and the ways in which I lived out my calling. I think that by identifying solely as male, I tried to hide the more female or feminine aspects of myself in order to fit more easily into church and society. The problem is that doing that hurt me and limited my communication with others.

It isn't unusual for trans people to go through an ultra-gendered stage. As I have mentioned before, the incredible excitement of finally discerning your identity can lead to quick decisions and extreme binaries. The joy of being able to be seen as male made it impossible, at first, for me to discover what kind of man I wanted to be. It was easier to slip into a lazy, at times toxic, masculinity without stopping to think. Eventually, though, I was able to take a step back and work out who I really am.

So, I am Alex. I am trans. I am queer. My body is neither male nor female. And that is good. Mostly people see me as male. And that is good. I have a female history. And that is good. Sometimes I wear nail varnish. And that is good. I like to look different. And that is good. I like to be open about being trans. And that is good. I am listening, waiting for the next transformation. And that is good.

You see, I have been on a journey, and it is a journey to which many people, perhaps including my readers, would like there to be a fixed end point. It is easier to understand transness as a simple move from A to B. It would be easiest if I stated that I was assigned female at birth, felt gender dysphoria, underwent treatment and am now male. But that narrative is too convenient, too straightforward, too human and not spiritual in the least.

When I had been on hormones for a while, people started saying, 'Don't you look well!' with a tone of surprise. Whilst I was happy to take the compliment, I also realised that what they really meant was, 'Don't you look male.' And, similarly, any sign of femininity was seen as a problem or a sign of regret or weakness.

Those straightforward categories do not define me, though. Rather, my journey is about listening to God's call. And God has called me by name, 'Alex'. God has called me to undergo medical treatments that have healed my body. God has called me to let go of gender stereotypes and constructs and, instead, to believe that I am enough and that, by living in a state of flux, I can listen to that still small voice and go where I am led.

Much of the press and publicity about trans people focuses on binary identities, on the good news story of the unhappy man who has been transformed into a happy woman and vice versa. But what about those of us for whom the story is less straightforward? Non-binary* trans people aren't confused or messed up. We are simply continually open to being called somewhere else. And I think that is good.

Many trans people are seen as de-transitioning or regretting transition if they/we take any step 'backwards'. But, I think, that is just a narrow understanding of being trans. It isn't a journey in one direction; rather it is an ongoing consideration of and willingness to redefine who you are, who I am. I don't have any regrets and I haven't de-transitioned. I am just more open now about my full, trans self.

I have also found that being open about my non-binary identity has helped others to be open about their identities, and about their understanding of God.

I was asked to be a stand-in minister for a week at a small rural chapel, and was encouraged to avoid talking about being trans, but, ever true to myself, I ignored the advice and came out in my Sunday morning sermon. It turned out that one of the five people there was trans. The Spirit moves in amazing ways, does it not?

That person and their friend came back to see me on the Wednesday of my week there, and we spent hours talking. They told me that they had never expected to see another trans person in their rural town, let alone in the Church. We had a lovely, moving, funny, affirming conversation; each seeing and hearing the other in genuine fellowship. That person had felt entirely alone in their transness until they met me. Until I was open about who I was.

And what about people who aren't trans? I preached about LGBT+ identities for a small, elderly congregation a few years ago. After the service, a lady in her 90s, whom I thought I knew well, came to me with tears in her eyes. She said, 'I'm not sure if I believe in heaven. Is that OK?'

I hadn't preached about heaven explicitly, so her question was off at a complete tangent. Or was it? My decision to be open about who I was, and the necessary flexibility involved, showed her that it was OK to have doubts, to be unsure, to question tenets that she had been taught her whole life were correct.

Accepting and talking about transness isn't just about trans people, or about the changing world or the younger generation. Rather it allows people of all backgrounds, ages, and identities to question the things that they have been taught are black and white, freeing them from the chains of persecution, abuse and binary thinking.

I wonder what chains are holding you captive?

Feeling free on the beach in Scarborough.

Questions for reflection

- Who are you? No, really. Who are *you?*
- What truths do you hide because they might be inconvenient to others?
- Do you truly love yourself?
- If not, what steps might you take to care for you?

Activity – warm fuzzies

This is an activity that I learned as a youth worker, and have used successfully in youth groups, churches, corporate offices, conferences and hospitals. It works in all sorts of settings, because everyone needs love, affirmation and recognition.

There are lots of ways to do warm fuzzies, but this is the most straightforward:

- Everyone sits in a circle. Each person needs a sheet of paper and a pen. Ask each person to write their name on the top of the sheet of paper. Then pass the papers around, asking each person to write something positive about the person named at the top, until the paper comes back to the person.
- This should be anonymised, so that the commenters do not feel limited in what they might write.

Prayer

Sit before God and simply be.
Allow God's warmth, acceptance and love to inhabit your being.
Hear God's affirmation.
God beholds God's creation and says, 'You are good. You are very good.'

Travelling together

If I have the gift of knowing exactly who I am called to be, but do not have love, I am nothing. Love always protects, always trusts, always hopes, always tries again.

I know only in part, but when we are complete, what is in part disappears. When I was a child, I talked like a child, I thought like a child, I reasoned like a child. When I became who I am today, I put the ways of childhood behind me.

And now these three remain: faith, hope and love. But the greatest of these is love.

(Inspired by 1 Corinthians 13)

I have written, throughout this book, from my own perspective. Whilst I have tried to be sensitive to the voices, opinions and feelings of others, I can only write my story as I remember it, and as I live, and have lived, it. I am acutely aware, though, that we often fail the families, friends and loved ones of trans people. We don't give them space to tell their stories, express their feelings or work through their own transitions, which are part and parcel of loving a trans person. In this chapter, then, I give space to some of my loved ones to tell their stories.

I asked my mum, Pam, and my wife, Jo, some questions about their experiences of my transness, and have converted their answers into narrative form. I have anonymised some of their text and will respond briefly at the end of each narrative but, for the most part, I will let them speak for themselves. They have read through this chapter and agree that I have represented their voices fairly.

So, first, let's hear from my mum:

'When you came out it was traumatic, but for many reasons – not just the fact that you came out! I was 'absent', away on holiday in the US with family members. Dad phoned and said that you had 'demanded' to be referred to using male pronouns and that you wanted to be called Alex. I then had to phone your sister and feed her a lie because I didn't want to tell a 14-year-old over the phone that she now had a brother rather than a sister! Then I had to 'enjoy' the rest of my holiday as if nothing had happened and everything was fine.

The worst thing of all was finding out the way I did – over miles and miles – and not being able to see you or speak to you and know that you were OK. So, my overwhelming memory was upset that had little to do with your actual coming out and more to do with managing the circumstances around it.

I have to admit that I was quite angry at you at the time because of the timing more than anything. I had only just recently come out as gay and, inevitably, some folk were pointing the finger at me and 'blaming' me for being a bad mother and concluding that you were just a mixed-up product of my bad parenting.

I do also remember being absolutely terrified, a few weeks later, when I drove you to take part in a gathered orchestra course, leaving you there as Alex when you'd registered for the course in your previous name. I didn't know these people at all and felt you were very vulnerable. I felt so conflicted, as a mother, leaving you with strangers at that particular time in your life. I was worried about what clothes you had, would you pass, would they take you seriously, would they view you as a high-maintenance teen with mental health issues, etc …

My only reassurance was that, even if all that were true, your musical ability and your lovely personality should help them warm to you. But I still remember walking out of the place I left you in, back to the car for a long, lonely drive home, and wondering if you'd be OK.

There were possibly signs when you were growing up that you might be trans, though I didn't recognise it at the time. You were always serious – both as a baby and as a young child. Always a wee bit reticent and unsure. Not really withdrawn, just sort of puzzled. Maybe some inner part of you was feeling 'out of sync' with your outer experience? You never said or did anything to suggest inner turmoil so, perhaps, it was more a subtle imbalance that was affecting you?

Perhaps the fact that your primary two teacher told us, at a parents' evening, that you were socially isolated and sat by yourself on a playground bench playing the recorder at lunch time was a clue that you didn't really find life at an all-girls' school very easy.

I also remember a big argument between you (aged about ten) and your sister (aged about seven) at GAP. I'd told you to go and choose a fleece hoodie each whilst I browsed the sale. The hoodies were arranged on two circular display tables, one table sporting what were typically viewed to be 'girly' colours and the other more 'boyish' ones. Your sister came looking for me, clutching her customary choice of some shade of purple. She accused you of choosing from the 'wrong' table. You then appeared with a dark grey hoodie with navy letters. She said it was for a boy, you argued that you didn't care, and you liked it. I remember thinking that I liked it better than the 'girlish' ones, too. I told her off and you got your grey hoodie. A few weeks later, we attended a party for a friend. Years later, I saw a photo taken at the party. You were standing off to the side, apart from the other children, leaning against a wall. You didn't really look sad, you just looked separate from them.

You were wearing jeans and the grey GAP hoodie.

When you moved to a mainstream school, you complained about missing the rigidly predictable uniform of your previous school, because you said you didn't know what to wear. You always asked me to do your hair and sought advice from your sister regarding clothes and makeup for secondary school.

Your haircuts got progressively shorter. I remember you walking towards me when you'd been to get your hair cut without me for the first time. You had a friend with you for moral support. You'd had your hair cut quite short. In fact, the hairdresser later confessed to me that she was worried, as she was cutting it, that I wouldn't be happy! I just remember you looking so happy as you walked towards me and thinking how well it suited you. After that, each haircut was progressively shorter, and I now often wonder, when I look at photos, if you knew already but didn't quite understand what it was.

Faith wasn't a factor in how I saw your trans identity when you first came out. Now, I'm extremely proud of the niche you've managed to carve for yourself, as a veritable guru on all things related to queer theology. I do sometimes worry that your obvious stature/high profile as an 'expert' in this area causes you to be more vulnerable/open to adverse attention. But I'm not consumed by it. I'm more grateful and proud that you have found passion and purpose in the work that you do and that others are recognising your gifts.

One of the hardest parts of your transition was being so far away and wondering/worrying if you were ok. The magazine article that you wrote in early transition remains one of the toughest things that happened. You believed that my angst was related to you being trans. It wasn't. It was about your lack of forethought in relation to self-respect, dignity and integrity and your inability to consider the possible wider impact of your actions on your family, especially your grandparents.

I was worried about the quality of care you were receiving and the hormone treatments. I researched the Gender Identity Clinic (GIC) and anything I could find about ftm transition*. It was scary, worrying about your physical and mental well-being. But it was also reassuring that the GIC seemed to have a great reputation. I was also confident that you would employ both intellect and caution as you were extremely bright and, also, hated being unwell. I had a friend at the time whose child was living/studying in USA when they came out and was self-injecting T* that they purchased online. I felt reassured that yours was a much more sensible, structured and monitored approach. She was envious of my situation with you and felt her worries were so much bigger than mine. I had to agree.

I also really struggled/still struggle with guilt over my late partner's reaction to your coming out and her refusal to allow you to stay with us because of her child. I'm so very grateful for the amazing relationship that has grown between you and my current partner. If I could turn back time, I would want you to know/feel that you were and always will be my first priority.

My relationship with religion is complicated. I have left the church but have also repeatedly been reminded that the church's ways and its rituals are buried in my very psyche, part of who I am. Particularly the words and the music. I cannot hear certain prayers/creeds/hymns without getting a lump in my throat. I really do, on some level, identify with it. But I have unpleasant feelings too. I find myself wanting and not wanting to return in equal measure.

I suppose, ultimately, your acceptance into and success in the church and your own particular brand of theology has given me comfort and reason to believe that there is room for everyone in the church (well, some churches!). My experiences with you (and Jo) in church have only ever been pleasant, positive and uplifting. Your talk at Jo's ordination/induction lives on as one of my most favourite sermons of all time. I'm proud that you are pushing the boundaries of theological rhetoric and that there are folk listening and valuing what you write and say. Who knows what the future holds for me in terms of the church?

Mostly, because I have been completely transparent and open about you being trans, the people who matter in my life are hugely supportive of my having a trans child. Your sister has been the same. I'm extremely proud of you and don't hesitate to share that fact far and wide! There are some who tell me that we are an amazing family and that I'm an inspirational mum. I'm not sure that's necessarily always the case! But, that's how I met one of my good friends, who is also the parent of a trans person. It makes me feel proud and also affirms for me that I am being true to the type of person I hope/want to be. In other words, if others can see it in me then I must be doing OK. I know there are, inevitably, some who must talk when I'm not around, but they don't matter to me so it's all good. I've certainly not lost anyone important and I've definitely gained respect and a few new friends too.

There have been some awkward moments with people I'd call churchgoers rather than Christians. Folk I've met at the shopping centre who were members of your dad's old church insist on referring to you by your former name, even though I'm pretty sure they know who you are. Another church family stumbled a lot in conversation when we saw them at the concert hall. The whole of our family was there, in bits and pieces, but all getting along really well. They had no idea what to say. They repeatedly misnamed you and stumbled along, finally ending with 'My goodness, you've had a lot of change to deal with!'

Then there's my evangelical friend who admires/respects me pro-fessionally but has no idea how to approach either your or my personal lives. She does try hard, though, and I respect that.

Your transition probably has affected how I think about gender. I think I've become a much more 'fluid' thinker. I actually don't really think at all, to be honest. I just prefer to experience people as people, considering our connection regardless of factors that are commonly used to identify folk, like gender, colour, age, ability.

I would like to say to parents of trans people: Love your child. They are and always will be your child. Love them, value them, know them and keep them. Don't seek to change them. Remember that none of us is being true to our relationships with others if we seek to change who they are. Cultivate your relationship with them. See their wonderful strength and resilience.

When/if you are struggling, ask yourself this: Would/could you be happy without them in your life? Would/could they live as full a life without you in theirs? Also, seek help/support if you're unsure. There's plenty of support out there.

The best thing about you being trans is, quite simply, who you are. I love who you are. You are funny, loving, creative, intelligent, caring and quite simply amazing. You live your life bravely and boldly with a level of certainty about who you are and where you're headed. I feel your contentment with yourself. I know you're OK. I know you will continue to be OK. These things make me feel both happy and proud.'

***

Hearing about how my mum experienced my transition was incredibly moving. I feel proud and fortunate to have such a loving parent. I also feel saddened, as I explored a little in Chapter 5, by the ways in which I hurt my family – not because I am trans, but because I transitioned in ways that were sometimes very selfish.

The magazine article that my mum talks about is one example of that. It was very early on in my transition, and I was a bit short of cash. Rather than taking the mature option and asking my family for help, I responded to a magazine that had been hounding me for some months for my story. I thought that, as well as earning some money, I would be able to help other trans people.

In reality, the magazine edited my words in a very trashy way and persuaded me to give them photos that I shouldn't have allowed to be published. One of my biggest regrets about transition was allowing that article to be published. I had a tendency to leap before I looked, but this has mellowed out into a more cautious enthusiasm. I am glad that I have another opportunity to write about my story in a way that respects and honours myself and others more fully.

I am incredibly grateful for my family's support of me. Many trans people lose their families when they transition, due to ignorance, intolerance, hate or fear. I am so fortunate that my mum's main concerns were for my safety and well-being.

My wife, Jo, met me when I was a fair way through my transition. Let's hear from her now.

'I didn't know you were trans when we first met. I knew there was a trans person in your year group at uni, but I didn't think it was you. One of many incorrect, and blinkered, assumptions I had about trans people was that it would be obvious and easy to tell. If you had asked me, I'd have told you I'd never met a trans person. I'm pretty sure now I must have, but didn't realise it. My first impressions of you were that you were very young. I know now that in part that was due to your stage of transition.

I'm pretty sure I had never considered whether I would date a trans person. It would never have been a question. I don't think I ever really thought about trans people. My only image of a trans person was from drag acts. I've had male partners and female partners, so gender would not have been an issue, but if I'm honest my prejudiced assumption that trans people were somehow weird probably would have been. I had a few days to get to know you as Alex before any of that baggage kicked in, and I will always be grateful for that.

There were two main difficulties for me in dating a trans person. The first was me, the second was everyone else! I had been brainwashed to the idea that gender is binary. Therefore, you were male, and according to my brain always had been; both inwardly (mostly true) and outwardly (not true). So, whenever you mentioned ballet lessons, for example, my brain said, 'That's unusual for a boy,' and it would take a moment to remember you were raised and socialised as female. When I told your mum to bring embarrassing baby photos next time she visited, I saw a flash of something in her face, before I realised that they would not show a little boy with cars, but a little girl with dolls. I had to retrain my brain to think differently. I see it now with others; people who know you are trans but still say things like, 'Harp is an unusual instrument for a man.' I see their faces when the penny drops –

some laugh, and others cringe with embarrassment.

I also had to learn new ways of speaking. New terms like trans, cis, gender identity. I had to learn how to reference the past. Couples ask questions as they get to know one another ... but do I ask, 'When you were a little boy?' or 'When you were a little girl?' There was a whole new etiquette to learn too. Was it OK to tell my friends? What could I ask and what shouldn't I ask about your body and the physical side of transition? You told me not to google, and knowing what I know now, I am eternally grateful for that! You also gave me permission to ask questions and told me gently when I said something offensive. That is so important. Communication. Being able to ask without fear of offending or being laughed at.

Telling friends and family was an odd one. Most of our immediate friendship group at college knew, so it wasn't an issue straight away. You were still working out how visible you felt called to be when we first started dating. I didn't tell my best friend. You assumed I had and mentioned it over dinner, so I had to take her to the pub to explain! You weren't sure about telling my dad, and I insisted. He was awesome and had the least dramatic reaction of anyone ever. I may as well have been telling him you liked ketchup.

Once you had decided that being radically open and honest about your transition was something God wanted you to do, it got both easier and harder. In some ways being able to mention it not just to close friends and family made it more normal, but it did mean it permeated every aspect of life. There was no space to go and hide. It also led to more varied responses, my favourite still being the friend who totally missed the point and was curious why such a handsome man would want to become a woman. When to disclose also becomes an issue. You don't want to blurt it out the first time you meet someone, but leave it too long and it feels almost dishonest, considering that you are out. Where and how to disclose is also an issue. Dropping it into an online conversation feels wrong. What if the person has a bad reaction and you cannot support them? Doing it over a coffee feels better, but you have to be prepared for the follow-up questions.

With the exception of my dad and one or two others, almost all of my close friends at some point fairly soon after finding out ask questions, often extremely personal ones. Most people want to know about your genitalia. They often work around it awkwardly, asking what you have or haven't had done surgically. Some, though, ask outright whether you have male genitalia or what size is it or how does it work. I have never asked a friend about their husband's genitalia, and never would. I'm sure they probably don't ask their cis friends either, but for some reason your being trans gives them permission to ask! At first this was offensive and intrusive, but now I choose to find it funny, as, I think, do you.

I thought I married someone who had transitioned. Oddly the space I felt least comfortable in was with other partners of trans people. People living with a partner in mid-transition, who were riding the rollercoaster of emotions that brings. I felt blessed to have met you, fully formed as Alex. You had transitioned as far as you intended externally and were happily male.

None of this really challenged my faith or my sexuality. My faith was perfectly happy that God loves everyone. That everyone is made in God's image. I do not judge a woman who has had breast augmentation or a man who has had a nose job as interfering with God's creation. Why should I judge a trans person any differently? There was a small part of me that regretted not being there to support you, and not being there to experience the journey. Be careful what you wish for.

Then we had a series of conversations about gender identity. I wondered briefly and silently if you regretted transition as you talked, whilst painting your nails, about accepting and embracing your feminine side. These were fears I kept largely to myself. You began to move again on your journey, to use labels like gender-queer* and non-binary. Suddenly I had some of the experience of transition. A part of me mourned for the handsome man I married. Part of me felt very alone, and I needed my relationship with God to hang on to, to prop me up.

I wasn't alone because you weren't communicating with me – you were. I was alone because trans partners often end up playing catch up, as thoughts that may have been percolating for years are finally expressed. You had already had conversations with yourself and God. By the time the conversations came to me you had already realised that you sat somewhere on the male side of gender-neutral*. I was struggling to catch up. I am grateful for being there for that part of your journey, and for the understanding it gave me into what other trans partners experience.

My understanding of gender has changed massively. From a binary I had never questioned, to a spectrum with male and female at either end, to a nebulous thing that somehow whilst being extremely important is completely and utterly devoid of meaning too. You are Alex.

There are blessings in being married to a trans person. I realise now I am not completely gender normative. I was raised by a single dad and socialised in quite a male way. I am much better at boy stuff than girl stuff. I am not trans. I am, however, much more comfortable just accepting that I have male skills and hobbies, and not so worried about getting the female bits rights.

There is an old joke about it being good to marry a man with a pierced ear, because they've already experienced pain and know how to purchase jewellery. Being married to a trans person means being with someone who has thought way more about their identity than most people. Someone who knows themself well and is radically honest about that. Someone who has changed and doubted and lived in liminal spaces. Someone who accepts change and doubt. Someone who understands about menstrual pain, and bras that dig in, hormones and the pain of high-heeled shoes.'

***

Jo ended by touching on a point that is very important to me. Trans people have experienced living in more than one gender construct, and sometimes in more than one type of body. I do think that my experiences of femininity are just as valuable as my experiences of masculinity and that, as such, I have an understanding of, and stake in, feminism.

Unusually, though, my understanding of feminism is illuminated by both misogyny and misandry. Hierarchies and gender stereotypes hurt people of all genders.

I have experienced the good and the bad of living as both male and female, and that can make my understanding of Jo's life, and our conversations, really empathetic and interesting.

I think that, as Jo has expressed, the fluidity that is often a part of trans identity is particularly hard for families and friends. I am incredibly thankful to have a loving wife who goes with the flow, is honest about her feelings, and helps me to explore who I am, and who we are as a couple.

***

It has been incredible to read my loved ones' accounts of transition, and to understand even more about how they have felt throughout my transition. I wonder if it might be possible to create that kind of empathy for everyone?

With my mum sitting beside a Scarborough statue of Freddie Gilroy made by Ray Lonsdale.

Questions

- Is one of your loved ones trans or gender-nonconforming? How has it been?
- Which aspects of your family life are very hidden? Which are very public?
- Do you know anyone who is related to, or loves, a trans person?
- How might you support them?

Activity – letter writing

- Write a letter to someone you care about; a family member, partner or friend. Consider what you might tell them to help them to understand you better. Is there anything for which you would like to say sorry or thank you?

Prayer – based on the Lord's Prayer

Our holy parent;
hallowed be your name;
your kingdom come;
your will be done;
in transition, overcoming stasis.

Give us this day the strength to be honest.
And forgive us for words that have hurt others,
as we forgive those whose words have hurt us.

And lead us not into distrust;
but deliver us from separation.

For yours is the way,
the truth and the life,
today and always.
Amen.

With my wife, Jo, preparing to lead worship together.

Transforming community

And so we reach the end of this book and an oasis, a resting point, in this journey. There are resources on the last few pages that I hope you will want to explore as you continue to consider trans identities. For now, though, let's consider what we have experienced.

You have encountered, and perhaps reconsidered, scripture: from the Genesis creation narratives to the Psalms, from the Prophets to the Gospels. All tracing the story of a God who creates and re-creates each of us, calls us by name, and transforms us time and time again.

You have been asked questions about identity and gender, church and personhood – all tracing the story of humans: who we are, who *you are,* created and recreated, called and transformed. You have been introduced to, and have perhaps tried out, some activities: exploring the gendering of toys and magazines, the cross-roads in our lives, opinions and good disagreement, embodiment, conversation, affirmation and writing.

And you have joined me as I have told my story. From anxious girl to awkward boy to me. Just me. Alex. Trans. Christian. Human. At the heart of that story are communities. Families, schools, churches, youth groups, universities ... And so I wonder if communities are, in fact, the centre of this story. Not me, not gender, not Christianity but the communities that we dwell within and the relationships that we have a part in shaping.

To end, then, I would like to share some top tips for communities that would like to be more welcoming to trans folk. Life is, first and foremost, all about love; all about sharing together, breaking bread, telling stories, singing, celebrating. So how can your community better celebrate with the trans people in your midst?

1. Think carefully when citing scripture passages that have been used to hurt trans people and deny their personhood. An example is the Genesis creation narratives. Think and, if possible, talk with trans people about creative and respectful ways to read scripture.

2. Use inclusive language when talking about people. Phrases such as 'Christian men and women' exclude many trans people.

3. Some trans people (and people in general!) are touch-sensitive. Do not touch or hug a trans person without asking first.

4. Do pray with and for trans people, but remember that asking to or saying you will pray for a trans person can be a sensitive topic. Many trans people have had prayer used against them as a weapon. Ask people what you can pray about for/with them.

5. Remember that anyone might be trans, and that trans people have families too. Don't assume that trans identities are not relevant or personal for the people around you or in your congregation. Do offer pastoral support to the families, friends and loved ones of trans people, who might be experiencing things very differently from the trans person themself.

6. Consider offering renaming or affirmation services for trans people that give them an opportunity to celebrate their identity before God.

7. Don't just tolerate, accept or include; celebrate! Transgender. Christian. Human. God creates us in the divine image, God sees us, God blesses us and God says, 'You are good.'

It's as simple as that! I hope you have found the stories told here, and the resources presented, life-giving, affirming, helpful and interesting.

If you would like to know more or to join me on my continuing journey, please visit me at www.transgenderchristianhuman.com.

I started, and so would like to end, with some words from *The Gospel According to Jesus, Queen of Heaven:*

> *But I say to you:*
> *bless you if people abuse you or persecute you*
> *because it means you are bringing about change.*
> *And bless those who persecute you too*
> *because hatred is the only talent that they have,*
> *and it really doesn't amount to much.*
> *They will lose what little they have.*
> *And anyway change will come in the end*
> *and one day the world will be free.*
>
> [She lights a candle.]
>
> *And why do we resist?*
> *Why can't we celebrate?*

Resources

Defining terms

Here you can find the definition of terms marked with a star in the main text of this book.

Advocates speak up for trans rights in the public square.

Allies, in this context, are those who support trans people.

Binding (to bind) is a form of impermanent chest flattening used by transmasculine people. Safe binding is performed using specially designed compression vests. Some people, often due to financial need, bind unsafely using various materials including tape.

Bisexual is a sexual identity which refers to those who are attracted to men and women.

Cis (cisgender) refers to someone whose gender identity correlates with their gender assigned at birth.

Doxing is publishing private information about a person. Trans people are often doxed by the malicious publication of their previous name or old photos. The term 'dead-naming' is also used.

Drag refers to the act of wearing the clothing of a gender differing from one's own for performance purposes.

Embodiment refers to the state of existing in a body. All people are embodied. Academic discourse around embodiment focuses on elements of personhood – being human – that are specific to the state of existing in a body including, but not limited to, medical ethics, body image, gender, sex, sexuality, ethnicity, disability and so on.

FTM transition refers to a gender transition from female to male.

Gender assigned at birth refers to the sex that medical professionals and/or others designate a baby; usually based on genital appearance.

Gender dysphoria is a feeling of intense discomfort with one's body (usually relating to masculine or feminine attributes) or one's perceived gender or gender role, and can be medically diagnosed.

Gender-neutral is a gender identity label used by those who do not identify with gender.

Gender nonconformity refers to traits or actions which differ from one's gender assigned at birth or from societal gender norms.

Gender-queer is a gender identity label used by those whose gender challenges the norms of male and female.

The **Gender Recognition Act** (2015) allows trans people to seek a Gender Recognition Certificate, makes it illegal to out anyone with one, and offers trans people some legal protection from discrimination and abuse.

Gender Recognition Certificates (GRCs) are legal documents that allow a trans person to legally identify as the gender that they live as. Currently, in the UK, Gender Recognition Certificates only recognise the binary genders male and female.

Gender specialists are medical professionals including, but not limited to, endocrinologists, surgeons, psychologists, psychiatrists and counsellors who focus on the diagnosis and management of gender dysphoria and related conditions.

Identity is one's own sense of who one is and can be made up of a range of facets including, but not limited to, age, ethnicity, cultural background, gender, disability, sexuality and so on.

Latinx is a term used by people of Latin(o/a/inx) ethnicity who reject the gendered terms Latino and Latina.

LGBT+ stands for lesbian, gay, bisexual and transgender. The plus refers to those who might self-identify under the queer umbrella not represented in the acronym including, but not limited to, asexual, pansexual, questioning and so on.

Marry, in this context, refers to the legal action in which a person takes another person as their spouse. Same sex and opposite sex marriages are defined separately in law. As such, a trans person without a GRC would be married as their previous gender whereas a person with a GRC marries as their current gender. Unfortunately, this affects the wording that is used in the legal declarations.

MTF transition refers to a gender transition from male to female.

Muscular redistribution is a biological process by which a person's fat and muscles are reshaped and positioned in accordance with the hormones prevalent in their body. For example, a person taking testosterone may notice a redistribution of fat from the hips to the stomach, or an increase in musculature.

Non-binary is a gender identity label used by those whose gender identity is neither (and/or both) male and/or female.

Pansexual is a sexual identity which refers to those who are attracted to people of all genders.

Peri-areolar mastectomy is a surgical technique whereby a surgeon cuts around the nipples in order to use liposuction to remove breast tissue. The incisions are then closed around the nipples using purse-string sutures. This technique is most successful in individuals with a relatively small chest.

Phantom pain is physical pain felt for psychological reasons and can be a symptom of gender dysphoria.

Queer is a term that has historically been used against LGBT+ people and is now being reclaimed as an identity label that can be used by those who don't feel that they are represented by other terms. Queer should only ever be used by a person who identifies as such and should not be used to refer to someone else unless it is the term that they ask you to use.

Self-harm is the act of intentionally hurting or neglecting oneself, usually in order to relieve psychological pain.

T is short for testosterone, the masculinising hormone.

Trans is short for transgender and is thought of, by some, as more inclusive of those who do not relate to gender at all.

Trans theology is a branch of queer theology concerning trans identities and theological anthropology (the study of personhood in relation to God).

Transgender is an umbrella term referring to all those whose gender identity differs from their gender assigned at birth.

Transition is the process through which a trans person begins to live in their genuine gender identity. It might include changing one's name and pronouns, having medical treatment, making changes in one's appearance and coming out.

Transman refers to someone who has transitioned from female to male.

Transwoman refers to someone who has transitioned from male to female.

Who am I?

This is a prayer activity which enables reflection and discernment regarding one's identity.

As well as this prayer, you will need a quiet, calm space, some paper and pens, pencils or creative media of your choice and some time to explore.

God of nurturing love,
you have searched me and known me;
even that which I have hidden is known to you.
Help me to listen to your call on my life.

Lift up your hands and look at them. Really look. Explore your tendons and bones, veins and freckles, scars and marks. Try to count the hairs on a finger or study a nail in some depth. Close your eyes. Run your hands over each other, feeling their unique shape and the texture of your skin.

God of creative power,
you created these hands so that I might create
even that which seems impossible,
even that which I cannot understand.
Help me to draw out your call on my life.

Pick up a pencil and draw yourself in ten years' time. Don't worry about how good it is, or how realistic. Just spend some time with God thinking creatively about who you want to be. If you are struggling to start, how about beginning with a haircut or some clothes? Who are you? Who is God calling you to be?

God of transforming possibility,
you transformed my vision so that I might understand
who I am, who I can be, who I will be with your support.
Stay with me as I continue to discern my identity.
Grant me strength and courage as I move forward,
and wisdom as I seek your will.

Amen.

If you would like to seek support as you discern a call to transition, find a support group that suits you at
https://www.allabouttrans.org.uk/support-organisations/

If you are using this resource with a gender non-conforming child or young person, seek support from
https://www.mermaidsuk.org.uk/

If you would like pastoral support in spiritual discernment from a transgender Christian, please contact me via
https://www.transgenderchristianhuman.com/contact/

New life in you

This is a song that my wife and I wrote together which affirms the identity of trans people and might be used in a trans renaming ceremony. It is set to part of Beethoven's 'Pathétique' Sonata.

New life in you,
recreated and renewed,
Both chosen and desired,
in Christ a new creation.

Clay the potter threw,
reformed and shaped anew,
called to your service,
in Christ a new creation.

Drawn from life of old,
in your image manifold,
humbled by your mercy,
in Christ a new creation.

Given new heart,
by grace another start,
a life made for worship,
in Christ a new creation.

Called now by name,
released by spirit's flame,
to walk in your footsteps,
in Christ a new creation.

Prayers

In the beginning God created all things

In the beginning God created all things,
land and sea and the marshlands in between,
light and darkness and the twilight in between,
man and woman and those in between.
In the beginning God created all things in diversity,
with all possibilities in between.
At our beginning God created each one of us
and all our possibilities.

God of creation and change,
we thank you for calling us by name.
We remember how you changed the names
of many called to do your work.
Abraham and Sarah, Jacob, Peter and Paul
all journeyed with you and became new creations.
In renaming them you recreated their lives,
as you recreate us anew each day.

Prayer based on Jeremiah 18

Thank you, God,
that you make and shape us anew each day,
handcrafting every element,
forming us into the person you want us to be.
Thank you for our new beginning today.

Make us like fresh, moist clay,
not glazed and hard,
but soft and changeable,
ready to be reformed.

Raw clay from the ground is no good for pots.
The potter must labour to prepare it for use.
We thank you for the experiences that prepare us
for the journey that changes us.

We confess that sometimes we forget we are just raw clay.
Prepare us to be made useful in your service.
Wash us clean,
soften our hardened hearts,
so that you can sculpt us and mould us.
Forgive our flaws and remake us as new creations
moulded by your fingers
and call us back to life,
renewed, reshaped and recreated.

We give thanks that you are an artist
who always sees the creative possibilities
in these lumps of imperfect clay.

A prayer for a parent

Loving God,
I mourn for the child I have lost,
and I know you mourn with me.
I mourn for the child I have lost,
but you tell me they are not really gone.

I mourn for the child I have lost,
but you show me they have just changed.
I mourn for the child I have lost,
but you tell me to celebrate.

I celebrate what my child has become,
and I know you celebrate with me.
I celebrate what my child has become,
but you tell me they are still the same.

I celebrate what my child has become,
but you show me they will still change.
I worry what my child may become,
but you tell me to trust.

The creation of the earthlings

From Genesis; translated by Alex Clare-Young

This re-imagining of the Genesis creation stories reconsiders the translation of gender.

Then God said, 'Let us make humankind in our image, according to our likeness; and let them have dominion over the fish of the sea, and over the birds of the air, and over the cattle, and over all the wild animals of the earth, and over every creeping thing that creeps upon the earth.'

So God created humankind in their image, in the image of God they created them; masculine and feminine they created them.

Or, put another way ...

YHWH formed an earthling from the dust of the ground and breathed into its nostrils the breath of life; and the earthling became a living being. And YHWH planted a garden in Eden, in the east; and there YHWH put the earthling whom YHWH had formed.

Then YHWH said, 'It is not good that the earthling should be alone; I will make it a partner to mirror it.' So out of the ground YHWH formed every animal of the field and every bird of the air and brought them to the earthling to see what it would call them; and whatever the earthling called every living creature, that was its name. The earthling gave names to all cattle, and to the birds of the air, and to every animal of the field; but for the earthling there was not found a helper that mirrored it.

So, YHWH caused a deep sleep to fall upon the earthling, and it slept. Then YHWH took one of its sides and closed up its place with flesh. And the side that YHWH had taken from the earthling YHWH made into another living being and brought it to the earthling.

Then the earthling said, 'This at last is bone of my bones and flesh of my flesh; this one shall be called (Wo)man, for out of (Man) this one was taken.'*

---

* The brackets here indicate the wordplay of forming the word 'man' out of the word 'wo-man', highlighting the similarities between the two humans, rather than the differences.

Transgender Day of Remembrance

This is an act of remembrance and a sermon that I presented on Transgender Day of Remembrance (TDoR). It may be useful for others preparing for a similar service.

Memorialising

Draw or paint a cross on a large canvas. Prepare, and attach with Blu Tack, clusters of paper leaves. Each leaf can bear the name of a trans person whom you are memorialising.

Isn't this tree beautiful? It is adorned with the names of the *(insert number)* transgender and gender-nonconforming individuals who have been murdered this year. You also have a blank leaf, that you received as you came in today. That leaf memorialises the *(insert number)* unnamed trans people who were killed this year, as well as those who have died as a result of suicide.

Take it home with you and colour it in, as you reflect on today.

Our act of remembrance will help us to recognise and witness to the fact that the world is a less beautiful place without them. We will take their leaves away and be left with a bare tree of life.

This isn't an easy remembrance; it is tough. As we remember them, we are confronted with the reality of their absence.

During a time of quiet, I would like to encourage you to come up and remove clusters of leaves from the tree. Take them away with you to help us as we continue to remember. We will keep removing leaves until the tree is bare.

You will also find a booklet beside the tree with a list of names. Please only take one if you feel that it will be safe and helpful for you to do so.

Once all of the leaves are gone, we will conclude with a prayer.

Let's remember them.

Heavenly creator and parent,

As we look at this bare tree, and the leaves in our hands,
we recognise the tragedy of each death,
the stripping away of lives that leads us back to the cross.

May the diverse and courageous individuals and communities that we
commemorate today be remembered for their lives as well as their
deaths.

May those who mourn be comforted by the hope of new life, of trans-
formation, of a better world.

May we be some of those who co-create, with you, new life, trans-
formation, a better world.

Fill our lives, our communities and this world with hope, peace and
love, and strengthen us as we continue our lives in the service of your
values. Amen.

Sermon (2 Samuel 1.4-20, Mark 13.1-8)

This is but the beginning of the birth pangs …

I wonder how the miraculous and apocalyptic birth pangs that we
heard about in our readings can speak to us today, as we remember
all of the trans and gender-nonconforming folk who have been
killed in the past year.

This is but the beginning of the birth pangs …

Many experience their transition as God's answer to their prayers. In our reading from Hebrew Scripture, Hannah's birth pangs, and the arrival of the child whom she names Samuel, are God's answer to her prayers. In our Gospel reading, though, Jesus speaks of a different kind of birth pang: he speaks of a time of crisis; of war, of earthquakes and of famine, followed by, the reader assumes, the destruction of the earthly temple and the creation of a new world.

I wonder, then, if it might help us to consider the binary systems that trap, belittle and sometimes kill transgender people as being a bit like the temple. They are part of an old world order in which rules and regulations, buildings and money are more important than people, than peace, justice, truth and love.

This restrictive world order is the reality that trans people live in today; and it feels an awful lot like the beginning of birth pangs – although it is hard for many of us to tell whether we are awaiting a new, fairer world or just more hate and discrimination.

In our media-driven world, trans peoples' identities, and therefore our rights, are positioned as a matter of debate. Our new-found prominence in the public square has led to many people who struggle to understand trans identities choosing to state simply and loudly that they do not exist.

People are regularly given platforms, by media outlets, venues and even the government, to say that trans people do not exist. Further, the media regularly propagate the lies that trans people are, at worst, mentally unwell, potentially dangerous and sexually deviant, or are, at best, attention-seeking, medically-enabled, pathological liars. These are but the beginnings of the birth pangs of a crisis for trans people in the UK.

This is but the beginning of the birth pangs …

In 1 Samuel, we read of the persecution that Hannah experiences as a childless woman. The author writes that Hannah's 'rival used to provoke her severely, to irritate her' because she could not have children. Later, Hannah speaks of the effects of this provocation: 'I am a woman deeply troubled [...] I have been speaking out of my great anxiety and vexation all this time.'

Whilst the list of names gathered for the Transgender Day of Remembrance focuses on those killed unlawfully, suicide has also reached epidemic proportions amongst the trans community. This epidemic is not a natural part of being trans. Rather, it is a direct result of the persecution that trans people suffer.

Leelah Alcorn was a trans young person who committed suicide in 2015. In her note, she wrote that her mum 'reacted extremely negatively, telling me that it was a phase, that I would never truly be a girl, that God doesn't make mistakes, that I am wrong ...' Leelah's parents took her to religious therapists, who told her to repent for her gender-nonconformity and pray for forgiveness. She was actively and repeatedly punished for being trans and was refused access to medical treatment or appropriate psychological and social support.

Whilst Leelah was American, the suicide of trans people is a serious problem in the UK too. Research by Stonewall has found that almost half of trans people in Britain have attempted suicide at least once and 84 per cent have thought about it. This high rate is not surprising given that more than four in five trans young people have experienced name-calling or verbal abuse; three in five have experienced threats and intimidation; and more than a third of trans young people have experienced physical assault. Further, in the last year alone, two thirds of trans people have been discriminated against or harassed because of being perceived as trans. More than half of trans people have been told by their GP that they don't know enough about trans-related care to provide it.

We can, and should, do something about this. Hannah prays, and ultimately her prayers are answered. But, in the meantime, Eli supports her emotionally and practically, praying for her, speaking words of peace, and eating and drinking with her. It is not enough to wait for the birth pangs to be over. We need to work with God on this one. We need to support trans people. Listen to our stories, pray with us, don't let us be lonely – eat and drink with us. Find out what your GP surgery, school or workplace knows about trans people and encourage them to find out more. Contact your MP about trans persecution. Let's not just wait for it to get better. Let's do something about it.

This is but the beginning of the birth pangs …

We have already heard today about the unjust deaths of hundreds of trans people and are reminded of them by the candles on the screen, but injustice is more complex than a single identity label. The majority of the people whom we remember today are also female or feminine, black or Latinx, and lived in poverty. We must remember those at the intersections and at the margins, and work to topple the systems that are at the heart of their oppression.

Most of the transphobic murders that we remember today are set in cultural landscapes where gender nonconformity is feared, punished and, often, disallowed.

As the UK gender debate becomes increasingly hostile, levels of transphobic hate crime, the suicide rate amongst trans people, and even the number of trans people murdered, are rising at an unprecedented speed. This year we remember the murder of one trans person in the UK, and the suicides of several more. The number of trans deaths worldwide has increased once again, with Europe and the USA suffering significantly more deaths than last year. I wonder what the statistics will look like next year …

But it is also vital that we recognise our own culpability. It is racist and imperialist to judge other countries and cultures, many of which have gender nonconformity at the heart of their indigenous cultures, for the transphobia that has gradually arisen out of narrow white western ideals shipped out by missionaries and by politicians.

Jesus tells us that one day not one stone of the temple will be left upon another – all will be thrown down. Many believe that Jesus was talking about his body, but I like to think, as many liberation theologians suggest, that he was talking about rigid physical and metaphorical structures. That he was pointing out that all people should be able to worship in all places, not just in temples. And, similarly, that strict religious, legal and cultural regulations will not control people's lives for ever. The structures that we have helped to build need to be dismantled.

Trans deaths are a direct result of the rigid capitalist and binary structures that seem to control today's world. Perhaps our response as we remember those who have died should be a little less peaceful and timid. Perhaps it is time to start to work, as Jesus's hands and feet in the world, towards the destruction of these idolatrous and oppressive norms.

This is but the beginning of the birth pangs …

We know, as Christians, that the birth pangs of which Jesus spoke led to the cross, that oppression and injustice led to death. Jesus did not see oppression and flinch away, afraid. Rather, he chose to walk in the shoes of the oppressed, to speak up for them, and ultimately to be crucified for his radical views.

Earlier, as we memorialised the trans people who have been murdered in the past year, we stripped their names from the tree of life. A cross is what we are left with. This is what we carry. Before speaking of hope, it is vital that we take a moment to acknowledge the depth of our grief and despair.

This is but the beginning of the birth pangs ...

As I wrote this sermon, my internet browser alerted me that the list of names used today had just come out. I had hoped, naively, that there might be fewer names than last year. As you know, there aren't. There are many more. We Christians, not to mention Scots, are not always very good at recognising and sharing our emotions. But, in this instance, I think it is vitally important that I break down the barriers of professional distance to share mine.

As I write, newly reminded of what much of the world thinks of trans people, and acutely aware of the brutal and tragic loss of life, I feel many emotions. I am furiously angry. I am somewhat afraid. I am hopelessly sad. Whilst I recognise the complex circumstances that lie behind the names, I am drawn back to the reality that these are people who were killed for being like me. I am lucky that the extent of the oppression I suffer is difficulty in getting a job, the odd abusive comment on my blog, barriers to accessing healthcare, and friends who deserted me when I came out as trans. But today I am so aware that there are many individuals out there who think that those like me, trans people, should not be allowed to live.

However, as this sermon comes to a close, we must also think about hope. When the birth pangs come to an end, there is, we can only hope, new life. On the other side of the cross there is, we can only hope, new life. Beyond persecution and oppression there is, we can only hope, a new world order. I need hope. We need hope.

I don't believe, though, that this hope just happens. It is not a given. We are Christ's hands and feet and voices in the present. We need to be the bearers of hope. The bringers of new life. The messengers of love. Beneath all my negative emotions, hope blooms. Hope that is born of the transformation that I have experienced in my own life, and that I have seen in the lives of my trans siblings, including several members of this church.

Let's not get stuck at the cross. Trans people embody new life in a way that can inspire and challenge. We are creative, courageous, open, loving, genuine, honest and real. We are your siblings, your parents, your children, your lovers and your friends. We are here for you. We want to be beacons of hope. If you are trans, know that I see you and I value you.

So, I have a question for each of you here today. Will you be part of our hope? I hope that you will. Trans people are begging you to lend us your ears and your voices, to hear our stories and to share them, to pray and work with us to topple the walls that divide and control. To protest oppression, and to seek a new way. This is but the beginning of the birth pangs. Let us work together to create something new. Something better. Amen.

Further reading

Beardsley, C & O'Brien, M E (2016). *This is My Body: Hearing the Theology of Transgender Christians.* London: Darton, Longman, & Todd.

Beardsley, C & Dodd, C (2018). *Trans Faith: A Transgender Pastoral Resource.* London: Darton, Longman, & Todd.

Bornstein, K & Bergman, S B (2010). *Gender Outlaws: The Next Generation.* Berkeley: Seal Press.

Butler, J (2004). *Undoing Gender.* Abingdon: Routledge.

Chalke, S (2018). *The Gender Agenda.* London: Oasis Trust.

Hines, S & Sanger, T (eds.) *Transgender Identities: Towards a Social Analysis of Gender Diversity.* Abingdon: Routledge.

Erickson-Schroth, L (ed.) (2014). *Trans Bodies, Trans Selves: A Resource for the Transgender Community.* Oxford: Oxford University Press.

Feinberg, L (1996). *Transgender Warriors.* Boston: Beacon Press.

Feinberg, L (1998). *Trans Liberation: Beyond Pink or Blue.* Boston: Beacon Press.

Guest, D, Goss, R E, West, M & Bohache, T (eds.) (2006). *The Queer Bible Commentary.* London: SCM Press.

Gender Identity Research and Education Society. https://www.gires.org.uk.

Hartke, A (2018). *Transforming: The Bible & the Lives of Transgender Christians.* Louisville: Westminster John Knox Press. pp.3-4.

Mann, R (2012). *Dazzling Darkness: Gender, Sexuality, Illness and God.* Glasgow: Wild Goose Publications.

http://www.transgenderchristianhuman.com

Biography and contact

Revd Alex Clare-Young (they/them) is a minister in the United Reformed Church and an author, advocate and educator on transgender identities. As a transmasculine Christian, Alex is passionate about helping other trans people on their spiritual journeys and creating greater visibility and understanding in churches, communities, schools and workplaces. Alex graduated from the Royal Northern College of Music (BMus) as a harpist, before discerning a calling to ordained ministry of word and sacraments. They then worked in student chaplaincy for two years in Manchester, whilst applying to train for ministry.

In 2015, Alex moved to Cambridge to begin their training, where they met their wife, Jo. After completing their Bachelor of Theology for Ministry and Master of Philosophy through Cambridge University, Alex moved with Jo to Yorkshire, where Jo was ordained and serves as minister. Alex, who is also an Iona Community member, currently lives in Yorkshire with Jo and their Jack Chi, Digger, and enjoys walking on the beach, reading, writing, arts and crafts, eco-living and exploring. Alex currently works part time as the Community Leader of Peter's House in Hull, an intentional community of young adults who are exploring their faith and supporting local churches and communities. Alex also supports trans people and those who would like to better understand trans identities and is conducting doctoral research in trans theology.

If you would like to know more, or to get in touch with Alex, please visit their website: www.transgenderchristianhuman.com

Wild Goose Publications is part of the Iona Community:

- An ecumenical movement of people from different walks of life and different traditions in the Christian church
- Committed to the gospel of Jesus Christ, and to following where that leads, even into the unknown
- Engaged together, and with people of goodwill across the world, in acting, reflecting and praying for justice, peace and the integrity of creation
- Convinced that the inclusive community we seek must be embodied in the community we practise

Together with our staff, we are responsible for:

- Our islands residential centres of Iona Abbey, the MacLeod Centre on Iona, and Camas Adventure Centre on the Ross of Mull

and in Glasgow:

- The administration of the Community
- Our work with young people
- Our publishing house, Wild Goose Publications
- Our association in the revitalising of worship with the Wild Goose Resource Group

www.ionabooks.com

The Iona Community was founded in Glasgow in 1938 by George MacLeod, minister, visionary and prophetic witness for peace, in the context of the poverty and despair of the Depression. Its original task of rebuilding the monastic ruins of Iona Abbey became a sign of hopeful rebuilding of community in Scotland and beyond. Today, we are about 280 Members, mostly in Britain, and 1500 Associate Members, with 1400 Friends worldwide. Together and apart, 'we follow the light we have, and pray for more light'.

For information on the Iona Community contact:
The Iona Community, 21 Carlton Court,
Glasgow G5 9JP, UK. Phone: 0141 429 7281
e-mail: admin@iona.org.uk; web: www.iona.org.uk

For enquiries about visiting Iona, please contact:
Iona Abbey, Isle of Iona, Argyll PA76 6SN, UK. Phone: 01681 700404
e-mail: enquiries@iona.org.uk